Oxford International Lower Secondary

English

Workbook

7

Alison Barber

Mark Saunders

OXFORD

In this unit, you will practise the simple past tense, the passive voice, and the rules of direct and indirect speech.

Practising the simple past tense

Most of 'Morning in the desert' (on pages 5–6 of your Student Book) is written in the simple present tense. In the extract below, the original verbs in the simple present tense have been put in brackets.

- Fill in the gaps in the extract below by changing the verbs in brackets to the simple past tense. The first one has been done for you.

The sky _____ was _____ (is) pearl-grey when I ___________ (awake). My sister Phulan ___________ (pushes) me out of bed. I ___________ (tie) a piece of soap into the corner of my chador. I ___________ (pick) up two earthen pots and a padded ring to balance one pot on my head. My camel, Mithoo, and I ___________ (set) off for the water hole, the toba. Mithoo's small brass bell ___________ (jingles) cheerfully as he ___________ (moves) his head, impatient for me to fold back the reed door which ___________ (leads) from our courtyard to the outside. I ___________ (make) Mithoo carry the empty goatskin to the toba.

At the toba I ___________ (look) out over our dwindling water supply. Two-toed camel footprints ___________ (are) baked into the shiny clay at the outer edges of the toba. I ___________ (lift) my skirt with one hand, and the mud ___________ (squirts) between my toes as I ___________ (enter) the water. I ___________ (take) the filled pot to the bathing rock at the edge of the toba and ___________ (lift) my tunic over my head. I ___________ (throw) my hair forward and ___________ (pour) water over it.

The sun ___________ (edges) over the horizon. I ___________ (rub) the soap into my hair. I ___________ (squeeze) my eyes shut, letting the soapy water drain down my shoulders and neck.

The sun ___________ (is) extremely hot as I ___________ (walk) back. Over the next week we ___________ (watch) our water dwindle yet further. In the heat of the afternoons, before the daily wind and dust ___________ (arrive), we ___________ (dry) herbs. As the precious water ___________ (slips) away with the hot desert wind, we also ___________ (make) our preparations for leaving the toba and moving on.

Extension Write out all the irregular verbs in the past tense that you have used. These are ones that don't end in *-ed*.

Vocabulary

The vocabulary below is found in the extract 'Morning in the desert' in your Student Book.

● Match each word with the correct definition.

to yawn	plants used to flavour food
earthen	having a bright surface that catches the light
to balance	to open the mouth wide to take in air
brass	to fall slowly – usually a liquid, in drops
to dwindle	to cause liquid to flow out of something
shiny	to place something carefully so it does not fall
impurities	dirt or other unwanted substances
to pour	the skin on the top and back of the head
to trickle	metallic substance made from copper and zinc
scalp	to gradually become less and less
to rinse	to a very great extent
single	happening every day
extremely	just one
daily	to wash soap or dirt away with clean water
herbs	made out of earth or clay, often baked hard

English names

● List all the first names you can think of in English which are also a name of something in the English language. Think about things you find in nature, colours and gemstones.

Rose, Heather, Daisy …

Writing about similarities and differences

- Think about Shabanu and her life in the desert. Make notes in the Venn diagram showing the differences and similarities between Shabanu's and your own climate. Then complete the three statements in the box under the Venn diagram.

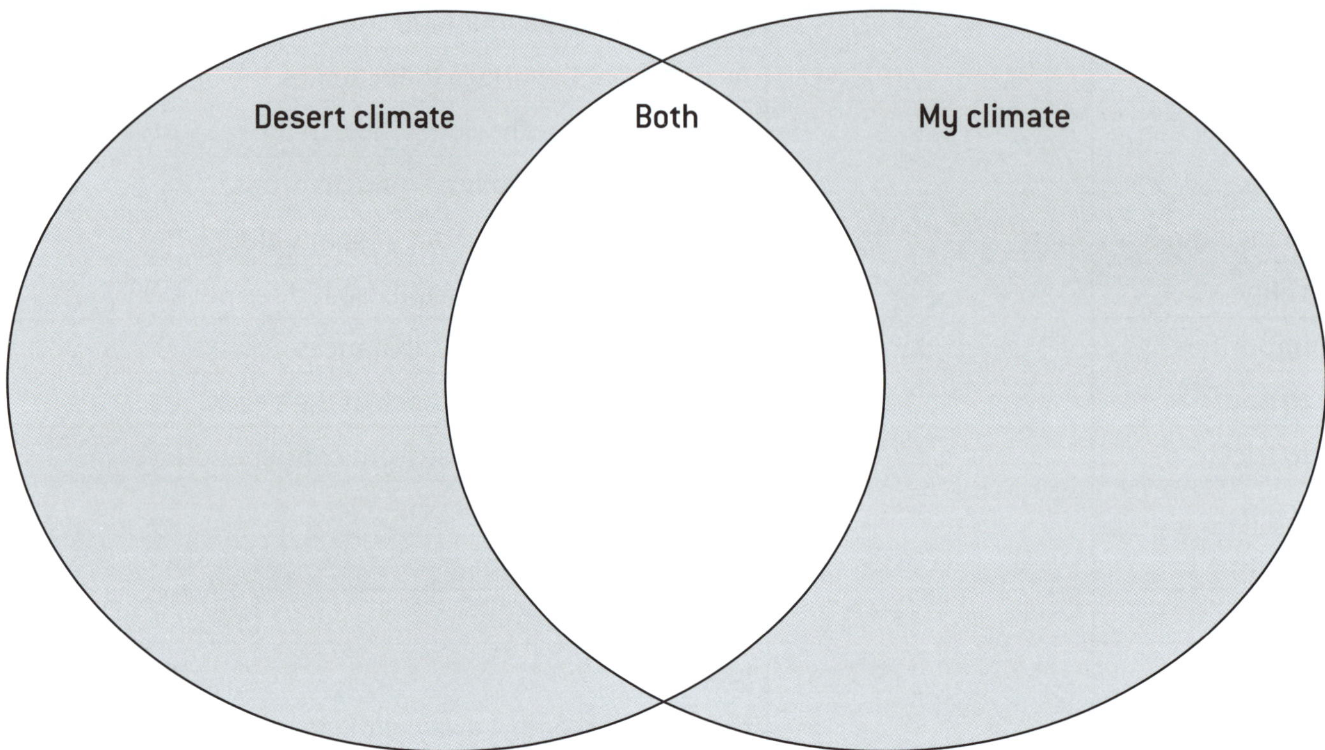

There are some similarities between the climate, scenery, and animal life where I live and where Shabanu lives …

However, Shabanu's climate, scenery, and animal life are different from mine in several ways …

In contrast, the climate, scenery, and animal life where I live …

Changing from passive to active voice

Think about the Carisbrooke Castle leaflet on pages 8–9 of your Student Book. Many of the sentences use forms of the verb 'to be' ('are', 'be', 'is', 'was', and 'were'), followed by a past-tense form of the verb to create the passive voice. For example: 'The well at Carisbrooke Castle <u>was dug</u> in 1136.'

The passive voice can be changed into the active voice by rearranging the order of the words. You need to add information about whoever is doing the action to the beginning of the sentence.

> **Tip**
>
> The **passive voice** is useful when you want to describe how something was done to someone or something, without saying who did it.

- Change the sentences below from the passive voice to the active voice in the past tense.

Passive voice	Active voice
The well at Carisbrooke Castle <u>was dug</u> in 1136 by the Normans.	The Normans <u>dug</u> the well at Carisbrooke Castle in 1136.
The main castle walls were built by Norman rulers.	
A wooden bucket was used by people to collect water.	
The treadwheels are still worked today by a team of six donkeys.	

The following sentences are related to the water wheels at Hama (page 10 of your Student Book).

- Change the sentences below from the active voice to the passive voice.

Active voice	Passive voice
You <u>can find</u> Hama about 40 kilometres from Aleppo.	Hama <u>can be found</u> about 40 kilometres from Aleppo.
The wheels bring up water from the River Orontes.	
Water fills and drives the wooden boxes.	
The people of Hama built 30 *norias* in the thirteenth century.	

Making a leaflet

- Draft ideas for an information leaflet about your home town, city or village.

Make up three possible titles for your leaflet.	 • • •
Use three facts or statistics to give your leaflet detail.	 • • •
Describe three things a visitor could do in your town.	 • • •

- Using the notes you made above, plan your leaflet below, showing the layout and images you will use as well as the text.

Extension Design a leaflet for a historic place you have visited or would like to visit one day. Make the most effective use of words, pictures, colours, and other design features.

Practising direct and indirect speech

The text 'The river gypsies' (pages 12–13 of your Student Book) contains examples of direct speech that use Babu's exact words. To report what Babu said, indirect speech would be used.

- Read the direct and indirect speech below and make notes on the differences in punctuation and grammar.

Direct speech: "My friend needs the snake catchers," Babu said to me. Indirect speech: Babu said that his friend needed the snake catchers.	
Punctuation differences	**Word differences**

Writing direct speech involves putting quotation marks around the words that are said. Indirect speech often needs the word 'that' to be added and pronouns to be changed.

Verb tenses are also changed when moving from direct to indirect speech. As a rule, direct speech in any present-tense form is changed into a past-tense form when reported indirectly.

- Change the present-tense direct speech examples below into indirect speech.

"It is fast-flowing water," said the police officer.	The police officer said that it was fast-flowing water.
"Cobras are usually venomous," warned the zoo keeper.	
"I am learning Chinese," replied the girl.	
"The old man has a snake in his house," Babu explained.	
"The weather has been terrible," he said.	
"If the earth smells of fish, then the men know there's a snake inside," Babu whispered.	

Extension Highlight the verbs you have changed in each example.

Writing an account

- Write an account, from Babu's point of view, of the river gypsies catching the cobras. Remember that Babu is quite knowledgeable about cobras.

Discussing a painting

- Reflect on your group discussion about the painting on page 17 of your Student Book. Fill out the table below to record examples of the ideas you shared. Use indirect speech.

Putting forward an original opinion	I said I thought the woman on the right was thinking about whether she should wear a hat in the sunshine.

Putting forward an original opinion	
Talking about what story the painter is trying to tell	
Discussing your own feelings about the painting	

Extension Highlight all of the verbs you have used in your account from Babu's point of view. Write down what tenses they are.

In this unit, you will practise the conditional, similes, and ways to write about the weather.

Creating a dramatic headline

Newspaper headlines often miss out words, usually the smaller ones. This has more impact, and saves space while communicating the main points of a story.

ARCTIC ICE ON THE RUN, SEAS ON THE RISE

HURRICANE MOST DESTRUCTIVE IN US HISTORY

FLOODS KILL OVER 600 IN HAITI

NIGERIAN HOUSES SWALLOWED BY SAND

EMPEROR PENGUINS EXTINCT BY 2100

- Cross out words in the sentences below to turn them into news headlines. The first example has been done for you.

> ~~Many~~ electricity companies ~~are set~~ to increase ~~their~~ use of solar power ~~methods~~.
>
> A newly discovered frog has been put straight on the endangered species list.
>
> The polar ice caps are melting and that will cause sea levels to rise.
>
> The most recent hurricanes are the strongest, and also the fiercest, on record.
>
> The northern hemisphere climate is predicted to become like that of the southern hemisphere.

Making a fact file

- Do you recall the fact file about polar bears on page 25 of your Student Book? Make a similar fact file about hedgehogs using your own research and whatever you remember from the article on page 23 of your Student Book.

Extension Write five headlines of your own about climate change.

Writing a newspaper article

- Choose an animal which is threated by climate change and write a newspaper article about why you think it is important to protect this animal. For ideas, recall the article you read on hedgehogs on page 23 of your Student Book and the polar bear fact file on page 25 of your Student Book, as well as your own fact file on hedgehogs from the previous page.

Tip

Use direct or indirect speech if appropriate.

- Plan the content of the sections and paragraphs of your argument below.

Introduce and explain the issues and the causes:

Provide evidence:

Conclude on what can be done:

Extension Write up a full, neat version of your article.

Reviewing vocabulary

The words below have been taken from the introductory text on flooding in Bangladesh on page 27 of your Student Book.

● Fill in the gaps, crossing the words out as you use them.

~~delta~~, desperately, flooded, frequently, glaciers, inhabitants, refugees, scientists, unable, vulnerable, worsened

---

There is a map on page 11 of your Student Book showing Bangladesh and its river

________*delta*________. Can you see why the country ______________ suffers from flooding? Bangladesh

is one of the countries in the world most ______________ to global warming. Floods have

______________ and the outlook is not good for the 150 million ______________, most of whom

are ______________ poor. ______________ in the Himalayas have melted, and ______________

say that Bangladesh may lose as much as 20% of its land to flooding by 2030. Twenty

million people ______________ to farm their ______________ land could then become

'climate ______________.'

Using 'if' clauses

In the composition 'The Best Day of My Life' (on pages 28–29 of your Student Book), Abdul writes 'If I miss school all the time, I will never succeed'. This is a conditional sentence with two parts. The first part begins with 'If' and is in the present tense. The second part is in the future tense and tells us what will happen as a result. These parts can be swapped over, for example: 'I will never succeed if I miss school all the time.'

● Complete the examples below to form full conditional sentences.

If the weather is good tomorrow, we will ________*have a barbecue on the beach.*________

If I save some money from my part-time job, I can ______________________________

If ______________________________, the animals will come out of hibernation.

If the Arctic ice melts, the polar bears will ______________________________

If ______________________________, we can cut greenhouse gas pollution.

If ______________________________, animals will get a shock when there are cold snaps.

If we all reduce our consumption, we can ______________________________

I will ______________________________ if I walk to school every morning.

If animals don't have enough fat reserves, they will ______________________________

Practising similes

Similes are used to add descriptive detail by likening an aspect of something, such as its size, to something else. For example, 'The creature looked <u>as big as</u> an elephant.'

- Use the words below to fill in the gaps to make some common similes.

a bird, a bone, coal, crystal, an eel, a feather, the hills, a rock, snow, ~~a wolf~~

as hungry as ___a wolf___	as solid as _______
as black as _______	as light as _______
as slippery as _______	as old as _______
as clear as _______	as white as _______
as dry as _______	as free as _______

- Recreate each separate simile and comparison from the poem 'Bush Fire' (page 32 of your Student Book).

a nasty rumour, an African summer, a cherry, flamenco, a cheetah, your lips, a Highland fling, lava, strip-the-willow, ~~a fox~~

as red as ___a fox___	faster than _______
as red as _______	faster than _______
as red as _______	as wild as _______
hotter than _______	as wild as _______
hotter than _______	as wild as _______

- Create some similes about fire by adding your own phrases below.

as fierce as ___a raging lion___	as bright as _______	as cruel as _______
as dangerous as _______	as big as _______	as destructive as _______

- Think of alternative similes and comparisons for these lines from the poem.

That fire, they said, was red as red as red as _______ ;

that fire, they said, spread and spread and spread, faster than _______ ;

that fire, they said, was hot, so hot, so hot, hotter than _______ .

Extension Create descriptions of fire using other poetic devices, such as words that rhyme or sound similar. Put these together to create your own poem about fire.

Vocabulary about fire

- Match up these nouns and verbs with their definition (meaning).

blaze	visible clouds given off by burning material
smoke	the visible part of a burning fire
inferno	powdery white or grey material left after a fire
to burn	to burn in contact with hot metal
charcoal	solid, black, burnt substance left after a fire
flames	a fierce, bright, glowing fire
to smoulder	fine black particles created by a burning fire
ash	pieces of hot material in a half-extinguished fire
soot	to burn and give off smoke without any flames
embers	a place of fiery heat and destruction
to sear	to be consumed by fire

- Now it is your turn. Write descriptive words, phrases and sentences about fire using some of the vocabulary you have learned.

Extension Think of an appropriate title that sums up your image of fire.

Extending weather vocabulary

- Match each of the weather words below with the correct definition.

frost	a season of heavy rains in warm parts of the world
icicle	covered over with clouds
downpour	frozen water droplets, especially on soil and plants
overcast	an arc made from bands of coloured light in the sky
sleet	a very heavy rainfall
monsoon	a small column of frozen water hanging downwards
rainbow	half-rain, half-snow
thunder	a snowstorm involving strong winds
hailstone	the loud noise made during a storm
cyclone	electrical charges from the clouds, visible as flashes
lightning	an individual drop of snow
blizzard	an accumulation of water over the land after rains
slush	a solid ball of ice that falls from the sky
snowflake	partly melted snow
flood	a storm where a powerful wind blows in circles

- Sort the words below into the correct category. Use a separate piece of paper.

typhoon, drizzle, frost, sweltering, clear, thunderclap, downpour, icicle, bright, blustery, overcast, breeze, sunshine, shower, snowstorm, heat haze, sleet, precipitation, thunder, monsoon, sunrise, cumulus, heatwave, rainbow, stratus, lightning, squall, hailstones, sunset, snowflake, damp, smog, cyclone, flurry, fog, blizzard, cirrus, tornado, flood, slush, scorching, hurricane, raindrop

Storms	Wind, clouds and sky	Snow and ice	Sun and heat	Rain
typhoon				

Writing a weather report

- Use the map below to pick a city and a type of weather that is different to your own.

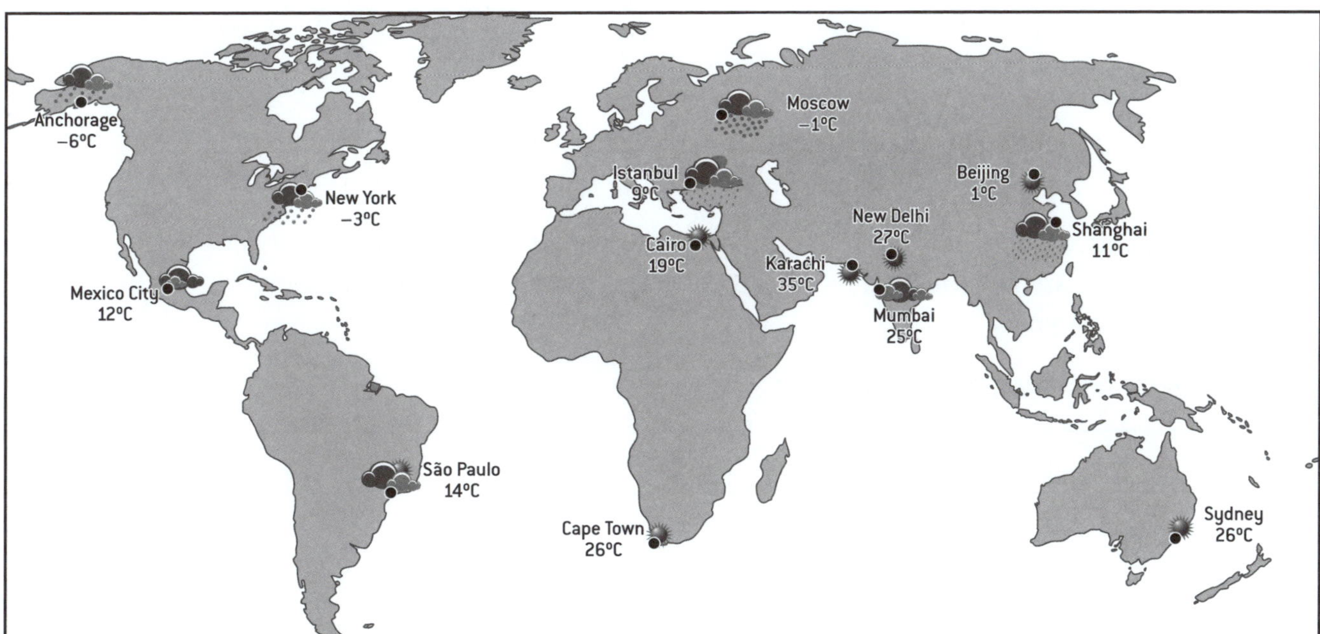

- Write your weather report in the first box below as it would appear in a newspaper or on a website. Then write out a script as if you were going to deliver the weather report on the television. Think back to the models of both types of weather reports provided on page 35 of your Student Book.

<table>
<tr><td>

Place:
Day:

Chance of ...

</td></tr>
<tr><td>

The day will begin with ...

</td></tr>
</table>

Extension Highlight the weather vocabulary you have used.

3 Air

In this unit, you will practise alliteration, noun phrases, multi-clause sentences, and comparatives and superlatives.

Alliteration

Alliteration is the repetition of similar sounds. You can use words that begin with the same sound, like 's', 'sh', and 'z', for example, to create a hissing or whispering effect.

- Put the alliterative words below back into the right order for the opening lines of the poem 'Can You?' that you read on page 37 of your Student Book. The first one has been done for you.

face, fingers, sell, slips, strokes, tangles

Can you _______ sell _______ me the air that _______________ through your _______________,

_______________ your _______________ and _______________ your hair?

- Identify the groups of alliterative words in each of the sentences below. It will help if you read the sentence out loud.

She decided to speak softly and whisper.	she, decided, speak softly, whisper
The wizard mixed a steaming potion.	
Lights shone fiercely on the empty streets.	
Raindrops splattered on the signposts.	
Swords clashed and spears flew swiftly.	
She sells seashells on the seashore.	

Vocabulary

- Match the following words from the poem 'Can You?' with the correct definitions.

to slip		value
to stroke		to move quietly, quickly and softly
perhaps		a long, thin piece of something
garden		an insect with large, decorated wings
worth		possibly, maybe
pure		a distance of about one and a half kilometres
butterfly		the covering to a building that keeps out the weather
strip		a pleasant outside space in which plants grow
roof		a small piece of something, cut from the whole
mile		to gently rub something, especially by hand
slice		natural, clean and unspoilt

Vocabulary to create mood and atmosphere

Look at this list of nouns and adjectives that could be used to make phrases to describe what you see, hear and smell in the painting *Landscape with Grey Windy Sky* by John Constable (on page 39 of your Student Book).

blue, copse, earth, fields, fierce, green, grey, heavy, patches, purple, raw, strong, threatening, trees, windy

- Add each of these words to the column below where you think it best fits. You may think some words could fit in several columns.

Sight	Sound	Smell	Mood
			heavy

Extension Find more words and phrases describing mood or atmosphere that could be used in a poem about air.

Noun phrases

Noun phrases can be very detailed and descriptive. In the extract 'Fog' by Charles Dickens on page 40 of your Student Book, several noun phrases are used to set the scene.

- Place the noun phrases below into the gaps so that the extract makes sense.

the eyes and throats of old men, a soft black drizzle, a sky of fog, flakes of soot, chimney-pots, the misty clouds, full-grown snow flakes

Smoke lowering down from ———————————, making ————————————

with ———————————— in it as big as ————————————

… Fog everywhere. Fog up the river … fog down the river … fog in ————————————

———————————— wheezing by their firesides … people peeping over the bridges

into ————————————, with fog all round them, as if they were up in a balloon, and

hanging in ————————————.

- Think of some noun phrases of your own using the lists of determiners, adjectives and nouns below. Draw lines between the words. Write your full noun phrases in the box below.

Determiners	Adjectives	Nouns	Noun phrases
the	sunny	truck	my rusty truck
one	bold	story	
a	broken	creature	
some	frightening	machine	
my	hilarious	day	
this	rusty	character	
another	tiny	place	

Vocabulary

- Match each word with the correct definition.

flakes	capable of causing damage, or hurting a person
fireside	tiny pieces of material, once part of something larger
to wheeze	the poisoning or spoiling of something natural
harmful	to breathe with difficulty, often noisily
pollution	an area in a room near a fireplace

Note-taking

- You have read the introduction to an audio tour for Angkor Wat (page 44 of your Student Book). Make notes below about your favourite place. Imagine you are making notes for the introduction to an audio tour.

Multi-clause sentences

Compound sentences are made up of several clauses. Usually, every clause is based around a single verb or verb phrase. A more complex sentence may include dependent sub-clauses.

- Divide the sentences below into their different clauses by putting a '/' between each clause. The first one has been done for you.

Access the enormous temple complex via the west entrance, **/** walking along a causeway that is guarded by lions.
Continue walking and in the centre of the temple you will find five towers
Be sure to find the carved wall friezes, including the *Churning of the Ocean of Milk*.
After visiting Angkor Wat, you must go on to see other sites

- Recall the text 'Protecting Angkor' on page 45 of your Student Book. Add one more clause to the sentences below.

The stone erodes <u>when pollutants come down in the rain.</u>
Electric buggies could be used at Angkor Wat ___________________________________
2.5 million tourists visit Angkor Wat every year ___________________________________

Extension Look for and note down more examples of compound and complex sentences as you read the texts in this unit.

Writing an email back home

- Imagine that you have been on a school visit to Angkor Wat. Write an email to your parents, carers or any other family member. Remember to use language that is suitable for the recipient.

  You could tell them about the view, the sites of interest, your favourite parts, and about protecting Angkor Wat.

- What photograph(s) would you attach to your email? Explain your choice.

Extension Draw a map to show your family members when you return home, showing your favourite places.

Comparatives and superlatives

Comparatives and superlatives are used to compare people or things. Comparative adjectives usually end in -er, or the adjective will have the word 'more' in front of it. Superlative adjectives usually end in -est, or the adjective will have the word 'most' in front of it.

- Join the adjectives below to the rule each uses to form the comparative.

difficult	Add -er to the end.
healthy	Double the final consonant and add -er to the end.
tall	Add -er to the end.
clean	Change the final 'y' to 'i' and add -er to the end.
wide	Use 'more' before the word.
big	Add -r to the end.

- Join the adjectives below to the rule each uses to form the superlative.

hot	Add -est to the end.
quick	Double the final consonant and add -est to the end.
extreme	Add -est to the end.
small	Change the final 'y' to 'i' and add -est to the end.
strange	Use 'most' before the word.
silly	Add -st to the end.

- Write the comparative and superlative forms for each of these adjectives.

Adjective	Comparative	Superlative	Adjective	Comparative	Superlative
nice	nicer	nicest	great		
smelly			fat		
unusual			easy		

Extension Make a list of all the comparatives and superlatives you can find in 'Something in the Air' (pages 48–50 of your Student Book) or in a chapter of a book of your choice.

Mystery vocabulary

The words below are often associated with mystery stories, or texts that describe something mysterious or unexplained.

apprehensive, chilling, eerily, to groan, mysterious, puzzle, riddle, secrecy, shadow, thriller, unexplained, unknown, to unnerve, unsettling, to wail

- Place each of these words into the correct category in the table below.

Nouns	Verbs	Adjectives	Adverbs
	to unnerve		

Planning a mystery story

- Finish the notes below for the different parts of a mystery story. The notes have already been started for you; you just have to finish them.

The setting: An old, disused warehouse …	The main character: A teenager who doesn't speak …	The main event: Strangers arrive in black cars for a meeting …
What is strange: A strange smell in the air …	The final outcome: The teenager speaks …	What remains unexplained: Where the smell came from …

Extension Research some mystery stories and find one to read.

In this unit, you will practise prefixes, relative clauses, possessives, expanded noun phrases, and slogans.

Emigrate, immigrate, and migrate

The words 'emigrate', 'immigrate', and 'migrate' are all verbs. They can be turned into nouns by adding *-ion* (instead of the final 'e') at the end of each word.

- Choose the correct word from below to complete each of the sentences.

emigrate, immigrate, migrate, emigration, immigration, migration

Enoch's family decided to ———————————— to find a better place to live.

The ———————————— official's job was to check the people entering the country.

Every year there is a mass ———————————— of mammals in the African Serengeti.

The company decided to ———————————— to a different set of software to save money.

When the living standards in a country fall, ———————————— often rises.

After studying there, I chose to stay and ———————————— to the UK for good.

- Use each of these six words in a sentence of your own.

emigrate	
immigrate	
migrate	
emigration	
immigration	
migration	

Extension Make a list of English words you know that have *ex-*, *e-*, *in-* or *im-* at the beginning.

Can any of these be used without the prefix?

Practising possessives

One way to show in English that something belongs to a person or thing is to use a possessive apostrophe: for example, 'Gita's glove' (the glove belongs to Gita).

<table>
<tr><td colspan="3">

Tip

Adding apostrophes will make a piece of writing shorter.

</td></tr>
</table>

- Add possessive apostrophes to make a complete noun phrase.

the rider + horse = *the rider's horse*	some girls + books =
my niece + school =	the boys + toilet =
a glass + contents =	James + hairstyle =
The Times + article =	a tree + branches =
some people + ambition =	the wasps + nests =

- Rewrite the passage below, rephrasing it to include as many possessive apostrophes as possible. You might need to change the word order in some of the sentences. Underline the word each time you use a possessive apostrophe.

> The new bicycle Inma had been given had a puncture and she was already late for the first lesson of the day. She borrowed the repair kit that her friend Marco had with him. He helped her remove the wheel of the bicycle and fix it, to the great relief of Inma, although he got grease from the bolts all over his hands.

Inma's new bicycle had …

Relative clauses

Relative clauses are a type of subordinate clause that add extra information about nouns.

- Highlight the relative clauses in these sentences from 'Shauzia's dream' on pages 56–57 of your Student Book (there may be more than one in the sentence).

> He also recommended her to his friend who had a grocer's shop, and she got a day's work there, cleaning the floor.
>
> She delivered trays of tea to merchants who couldn't leave their shops for a break.
>
> She couldn't go there often because the regular porters who were officially employed chased her away if they saw her.

Extension Write five sentences of your own that contain relative clauses.

Writing open-ended questions

Open-ended questions cannot be answered with 'yes' or 'no'. They require longer, more interesting, detailed answers.

- Use the following question words and nouns to create open-ended questions.

When / guitar	When are you going to play your guitar for me?
Why / school	
What / friend	
Where / England	
How / bicycle	
What / fruit	
How / horse	

- Now answer your open-ended questions with full, detailed, interesting sentences.

When / guitar	
Why / school	
What / friend	
Where / England	
How / bicycle	
What / fruit	
How / horse	

Extension Imagine you are going to interview someone famous. Write a list of three open-ended and three closed questions you would like to ask them.

Vocabulary about birds

● Match the verbs below with the correct definition in each case.

to flock	to pass closely over a surface
to hunt	to rest on a perch of some kind to sleep
to skim	to come together and act as a group
to gather	to become calm and still
to roost	to separate and go off in different directions
to settle	to track and kill
to glide	to come together, one by one, in a single place
to scatter	to turn suddenly, often to avoid something
to swerve	to travel through the air
to stutter	to fly through the air with little effort
to fly	to move in a circular motion, often around something
to swirl	to make several stopping and starting movements

● Write six sentences of your own using the verbs suggested below.

to flock	
to roost	
to swerve	
to gather	
to settle	
to stutter	

Extension Some of these 'movement' verbs have other meanings which are not connected with birds. Write out their more general meanings.

Expanding nouns

- Mariya Aziz expands nouns phrases in her poem 'Alien Abduction' on page 62 of your Student Book. This creates mood and feeling. Explain what impact the descriptions have on your understanding of the poem and what you visualize as you read them.

On a not quite round silver saucer	
A solitary world inside a world	
One of my kind	
A black-haired, brown-eyed Blot in a white sea.	

- Write your own noun phrases that include the nouns below.

world	
sea	
eyes	
day	
time	

Extension Find particularly descriptive noun phrases in a fiction book you are reading or have read.

Writing a letter

- Write a letter to your friend below, including three paragraphs explaining that you are going to emigrate to Australia. Use the appropriate conventions for writing a letter.

- Tick off each of the parts of your letter in the checklist below, when written.

☐	your postal address
☐	the date
☐	a salutation or greeting (such as 'Dear Malee')
☐	a sign-off phrase (such as 'love from' or 'with lots of love')
☐	your name

Extension Edit your letter to ensure you use both past and present forms of verbs.

Slogans

Organizations put a lot of thought into creating slogans to represent them to the public, or to advertise something. Slogan writers use language cleverly, including particular devices such as the use of double meaning, repetition, or rhyme to make the slogan memorable.

- Describe the idea or image created by each of the slogans below.

'Originals never fit' (Levi's jeans)	The product, jeans, are unique and individual and are not supposed to fit in with everyday thinking.
'Making the unmissable, unmissable' (BBC iPlayer)	
'Be humankind' (Oxfam charity)	
'Finger lickin' good' (Kentucky Fried Chicken)	
'A glass and a half full of joy' (Dairy Milk chocolate)	

- Write four possible slogans below for a poster advertising a holiday in Australia. Use some of the ideas from the slogans above to help you create several different ones.

Informal expressions

Common informal expressions are used in the text 'Grandfather's language' on pages 66–67 of your Student Book. These friendly expressions are used in everyday conversations and emails.

- Look at the expressions below and write their formal meanings next to them.

What's up?	
Step on it!	
I've got to run.	
It's a small world.	
Let's chill.	
Cool!	

⑤ Catastrophe!

In this unit, you will practise tenses, adverbials and the use of synonyms, similes and metaphors. You will also develop your writing and reporting techniques.

Technical vocabulary

When studying any discipline or topic, it is useful to know the technical terms.

● Match the geological terms with their definitions.

atmosphere	the outer layer of the earth
cone	the section of the earth's interior between the crust and the core
crust	the vapour or gas surrounding the earth and other planets
mantle	the shifting surface of the earth's crust
tectonic plates	the steep-sided top of a mountain formed by deposits from an eruption

Reviewing the simple present tense

Most of Pliny's text on page 72 of your Student Book is written in the simple past tense.

● Fill in the gaps with the simple present-tense form of each of the verbs in brackets.

Pliny _____orders_____ (*ordered*) ships to be made ready and they set out across the bay. He _____________ (*was*) anxious to save as many of the people living at the foot of Vesuvius as he _____________ (*could*). It _____________ (*was*) a great adventure to him as he _____________ (*was*) a keen scientist and he _____________ (*could*) observe the changing shapes and colours of the great cloud. Ash _____________ (*was*) now falling onto the ships.

As they _____________ (*drew*) closer to land, the atmosphere _____________ (*became*) darker and denser. Pieces of rock burned and blackened by the fire _____________ (*landed*) on the ships' decks. The sea _____________ (*was*) so thick with debris that they _____________ (*could not*) approach the land. So they _____________ (*sailed*) to the other side of the bay and into the harbour. Ships there _____________ (*were*) ready to evacuate the inhabitants. Broad sheets of brilliant flame _____________ (*were*) now lighting up many parts of the mountain as Pliny and his men _____________ (*hurried*) into a nearby house. Its floors _____________ (*rose*) and _____________ (*fell*) as ash and stone _____________ (*flowed*) beneath them. Then it _____________ (*was*) rocked by strong tremors and _____________ (*began*) to slide.

Adverbials

Adverbials are used in sentences to give more information about the time or place at which something happened, or the manner in which it occurred. Adverbials can be a single word or a phrase, and can appear at the beginning, in the middle, or at the end of a sentence.

- Underline the parts of the sentences from the Pliny text below that are adverbials.

Pliny ordered ships to be made ready and they set out <u>across the bay</u>.

Ash was now falling onto the ships.

As they drew closer to land, the atmosphere became darker and denser.

Pieces of rock burned and blackened by the fire landed on the ships' decks.

Its floors rose and fell as ash and stone flowed beneath them.

By the light of their torches, they succeeded in reaching the ships.

- Add an adverbial of your own choice in the gaps in the sentences below.

The space shuttle landed _after entering the Earth's atmosphere_ .

____ puppies love to play.

Glass breaks ___________________________________ but plastic is more robust.

The officer defused the bomb ___________________________________ .

___________________________________ the football team played much better.

Coastal redwoods grow ___________________________________ into the tallest trees.

The jockey won the race ___________________________________ .

A detective ___________________________________ checked the crime scene.

___________________________________ sharks scent blood from their prey.

Would you like to come to the cinema ___________________________________ ?

Pass me the scissors ___________________________________ and hold this.

Producing descriptive writing containing similes

- Write detailed descriptions of these natural catastrophic events. Remember to use similes in your descriptions.

Wildfires destroying large amounts of forest and scrubland.

An earthquake destroying buildings and roads.

A hurricane destroying shopping areas and schools.

An avalanche of snow coming down a mountainside.

Extension Add other types of figures of speech to your description, such as metaphors or personification.

Expanding sentences

Phrases give more information about, or modify, nouns and verbs.

- Make complete sentences using the nouns and verbs provided and by expanding them into phrases to give more information.

disasters / strike	Many natural disasters can strike suddenly without warning.
lava / flow	
atmosphere / fill	
ash / cover	
beach / run	
wave / travel	

Synonyms

Synonyms are words that share a very similar meaning. For example, the words 'fear' and 'fright' are synonyms.

- Draw lines to match up the sets of three synonyms.

awful		hazard		ascertain
immediately		bet		yield
find out		baby		terrible
gamble		promptly		straight away
risk		give up		magnificent
surrender		separate		danger
individual		dreadful		singular
brilliant		humorous		stake
infant		determine		comical
funny		tiny		minuscule
diminutive		glorious		juvenile

Writing a poem

- Use the space below to write a descriptive poem about a catastrophic natural event, using some of the vocabulary you have been gathering.

What causes earthquakes and tsunamis?

- Use the words below to complete the sentences about earthquakes and tsunamis.

tsunami, magma, plates, pour, upward wave, fault line, volcano, magma, mantle, volcano

Underneath the surface of the Earth is a layer, or _______________ of very hot rock.

Sometimes the Earth's _______________ slip under or run into each other. This can happen when there is a _______________ under the land or sea. If it happens under the sea, it can create a huge _______________, which becomes a _______________ when it reaches the shore. If it happens under land, it can create a space for _______________ to escape, causing a _______________ to erupt. A _______________ can erupt underwater too, causing _______________ to _______________ out above the water.

Extension Write a glossary entry for all the words you have added to 'What causes earthquakes and tsunamis?'

Story structure | You will need SB pp78–79

Many stories follow a similar general structure. They set out a situation where everything is normal (*exposition*), then something significant happens where the hero has to act (*rising action*), building up to a critical point in the story (*climax*). After this, the story moves towards an ending (*falling action*) and finally achieves a satisfactory conclusion (*resolution*).

- Fill out the space below with details from the story of 'Ningnong's great day' (pages 78–79 of your Student Book) to show how it fits into the traditional structure of a story.

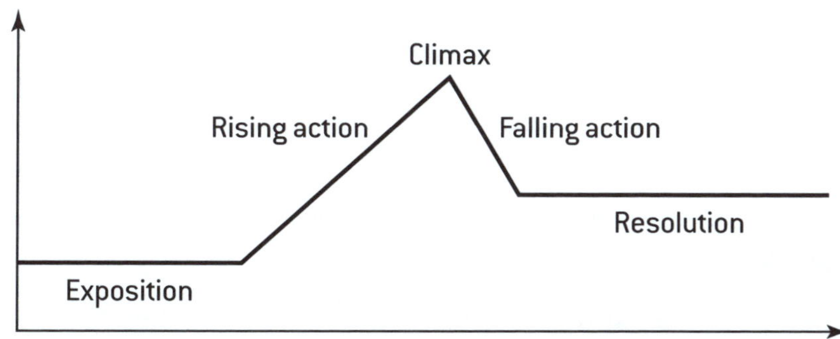

Structure	Details from 'Ningnong's great day'
exposition	
rising action	
climax	
falling action	
resolution	

Open questions

Open questions are types of questions that require a full answer. For example, 'Did you realize an earthquake had begun when the rumbling started?' is a closed question and invites a 'yes' or 'no' answer. However you could ask 'What made you realize an earthquake was taking place?', which allows the person to give a more detailed response.

- Write some open questions that could be used when interviewing Yong about how Ningnong helped to save the little girl.

How did Ningnong behave when the water disappeared from the beach?

Reflection on interview skills

When you carry out your role-play of the interview between the journalist, Yong, the little girl, and the tourists, plan ahead to make sure you ask good questions if you are an interviewer and give full answers if you are one of the interviewees.

- Once you have carried out your role-play interview, use the checklists below to evaluate the things you did well in the role-play.

Interviewer skills	Example
✓ Say things to encourage the interviewee	I made statements like 'You must have been frightened' when Yong paused.
☐ Use open questions	
☐ Ask follow-up questions	

Interviewee skills	Example
☐ Give extended answers	
☐ Be descriptive	
☐ Explain your personal view	

Extension Use a variety of question words to help you plan more questions a journalist might ask about the event, such as: 'where?', 'why?', 'how?'.

(6) Feeding the world

In this unit, you will practise proverbs, context clues, noun phrases, the simple present tense, and writing in the first person.

Proverbs

You have read on page 82 of your Student Book the proverb 'Give me a fish and I eat for a day; teach me to fish and I eat for a lifetime.' There are many more proverbs that are connected with food.

- Read the proverbs below and write an explanation for each of them.

<table>
<tr><td>It's no use crying over spilt milk.
Once something bad has happened that can't be undone, it is useless to spend time being unhappy over it.</td></tr>
<tr><td>Too many cooks spoil the broth.</td></tr>
<tr><td>If you can't stand the heat, get out of the kitchen.</td></tr>
<tr><td>A watched pot never boils.</td></tr>
<tr><td>Don't put all your eggs in one basket.</td></tr>
<tr><td>An apple a day keeps the doctor away.</td></tr>
</table>

- Choose one of the proverbs above and write a description of a situation to which it might apply. Relate it to something that happened to you.

Extension Collect proverbs from your own language and share them with your classmates.

Reviewing food vocabulary

The paintings by Arcimboldo, van Dijck, and Cézanne on pages 83–85 of your Student Book show several kinds of fruits, vegetables, and other food produce.

- Place the food that you saw in the paintings into the correct column. Add several more items of food grown or made in your own country. Some examples from the United Kingdom are listed below.

apricot, barley, butter, carrot, cheese, corn, cream, gooseberry, greengage plum, oats, parsnip, redcurrant, rye, swede, turnip

Fruit	Vegetables	Cereals	Dairy produce

More noun phrases

- Modify the nouns listed below by creating phrases around them that can also include additional nouns, adverbs, and adjectives.

apples _the sweet tartness of the under-ripe apples_

cheese ____

grapes ____

bread ____

wheat ____

Extension Describe some dishes made from the foods listed above.

Context clues

- Complete the table by writing definitions of the words listed. Use the sentences from the text 'A lucky day' (pages 87–88 of your Student Book) to work out their meaning from the context.

Word	Context	Definition
forage	Tree-ear was setting off in the early morning to forage in the village rubbish heaps.	to look for food, or for things of value
container	On the jiggeh was a large container made of woven straw, the kind commonly used to carry rice.	
glean	It would be many months before the rice was harvested and the poor people allowed to glean the fallen grain from the bare fields.	
oblivious	Oblivious to the hole in his straw container, the man continued on his way.	
ruefully	The farmer turned and saw the trail of rice. He pushed his straw hat back, scratched his head, and laughed ruefully.	

Story structure You will need SB pp87–88

- Fill out the space below with details of the story structure from 'A lucky day'.

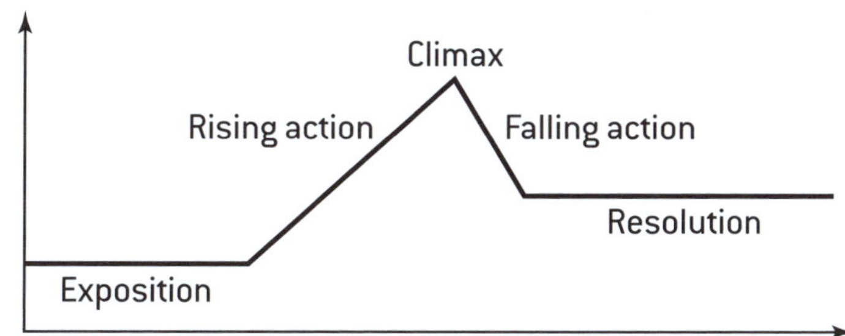

Structure	Details from 'A lucky day'
exposition	
rising action	
climax	
falling action	
resolution	

More noun phrases | You will need SB pp90–91

Noun phrases are made up of the collection of words that describe a noun or complete it in some way. For example, a noun phrase might be as simple as 'that apple' – the word 'that' indicates which apple is being referred to – or a long line of description, as in the phrase 'the sweet, succulent, rosy red apple'.

- Find examples of noun phrases in the reports about One Acre Fund on pages 90 and 91 of your Student Book. Use the main nouns shown below, and find the words around them that make up the full noun phrase.

maize	half a ton of maize
provider	
education	
house	
kitchen	
livelihoods	

Working on a farm | You will need SB p92

- Look at the information about Eco Fazenda Estrela on page 92 of your Student Book, including the advertisement and diary entries. List the different activities that happen at Eco Fazenda Estrela below.

- clearing a field for vegetables, using a machete
-
-
-
-
-
-
-

Extension Make up the longest noun phrase you can think of. Compare it to everyone else's in the class to see who has written the longest.

Writing in the first person

- Change the following report from the third-person plural into the first-person plural.

> The ecotourists arrived late at night and they were ready for their first night's sleep at the farm. A healthy breakfast awaited them in the morning after which they set off for the first day of their working holiday. Their day consisted of having to cut away at the undergrowth themselves; they thought it was very hard work.

We arrived late at night …

Agricultural vocabulary

- Match each of the words below with their definitions.

farm	an area where fruit trees are grown
organic	to collect the food grown on plants and in fields
orchard	to put seeds in soil so they will grow into plants
vegetable	natural, without chemicals
fruit	land and buildings used to produce crops and food
garden beds	the edible part of a plant, such as its root or leaf
soil	an area where crops are planted and raised
to harvest	an open space around a barn where animals roam
to plant	food grown on trees and plants, usually sweet
to sow	dung from animals used to fertilize soil
barrow	to feed on growing grass and plants
manure	earth containing enough minerals to grow things
barnyard	a container used in a garden or field, often wheeled
to graze	a very young plant, often ready to be planted
seedling	to put young plants in the soil to grow

- Fill in the gaps in these extracts from page 92 of your Student Book.

barrow, eco-farming, work, sand, regenerate, sowing, undergrowth,
over-farming, forest, clearing, bioconstruction, planting, sustainable, earth

Eco-holiday advertisement:

Here at Eco Fazenda Estrela, we are committed to _____________ farming practices

which will _____________ and restore _____________ land. Join

our _____________ team for a volunteering holiday and learn all you need to know

about eco-farming, permaculture and _____________.

David's eco-holiday diary: *Wednesday, February 16th*

After a night's sleep and breakfast overlooking the beautiful _____________ we

were ready for _____________. And what work! I can hardly lift my pen to write. All

day long we've been _____________ an area ready for _____________

and _____________. This involved cutting _____________ with a

machete, and carting away _____________ loads of _____________ and

_____________.

Eco- words

Eco- is used as a prefix in many new words to do with the conservation of
the environment.

- Use the examples below to fill in the gaps in the sentences.

ecology, ecotourism, ecotourist, eco-friendly, eco-design, ecosystem

_____________ is a branch of biology, to do with the study of the environment.

An _____________ is the complex system of animal and plant life that makes up
the environment.

David was enthusiastic about being an _____________, and wanted to take more
environmentally friendly holidays.

_____________ is a new form of tourism that supports communities and
environmental awareness.

_____________ often uses recycled or alternative materials.

_____________ products are made from sustainable resources like plant fibre.

Extension Can you think of any other *eco-* or agricultural words?

Writing about routine tasks

The poem 'Why the Old Woman Limps' on page 94 of your Student Book is written in the simple present tense. In each stanza, the first lines are written in the second person and the last lines are in the first person, but the main part of each verse is written in the third person.

- Rewrite the information about the old woman's tasks, changing it into the first person. Example: 'I milk the goat', and so on.

Third person	First person
She milks the goat, sells the milk to buy soap She goes to fetch water in the morning …	I milk the goat …
Goes to fetch firewood with her axe … Goes to the fields to look for pumpkin leaves … And hurries home to the children to cook	
Feeds and washes the children, and tethers the goat. In the evening she tells them all stories of old at the fireside	
She rests with the dark, at night she thinks of Tomorrow	

Writing about your routine tasks

- Fill in the boxes below with sentences about your tasks during the day.

 Write a poem about your daily routine and chores.

In this unit, you will practise sentence types, writing dialogue, the use of prefixes, animal vocabulary, possessives and determiners.

Sentence types

Sentences can fulfil four functions: they can be exclamations, questions, commands or statements.

- Match these four types of sentences with the correct sentence.

exclamation		Are you coming?	
question		You are coming.	
command		You can come!	
statement		Come here!	

- Identify the main function of each of the following sentences.

Have you ever seen the Colosseum in Rome?	question
Write the dialogue without using quotation marks.	
I didn't disturb them! Honest!	
Siberian tigers are now an endangered species.	
That was very stupid, Jacques!	
What animals have you seen in the wild?	
Once a tiger has killed a person, it is likely to do so again.	
Tell your group to ask questions.	

- Write a sentence with the function shown, using the word or phrase given.

basketball (question)	Do you want to come and play basketball?
my computer (statement)	
the night sky (exclamation)	
the police (command)	
a spare room (question)	

Writing dialogue

Look at the passage below, which shows direct speech and scripted dialogue.

Direct speech	Scripted dialogue
"I'd like to speak to you, Jacques," the safari guide called out. "Sure," said Jacques. "Is it about what happened?" he asked.	**Safari guide:** I'd like to speak to you, Jacques. **Jacques:** Sure. Is it about what happened?

- Convert these lines of direct and indirect speech into a sequence of dialogue.

"It was the best holiday I ever had!" Dani said.

Janis wanted to know what was so special about it.

"Seeing animals in their natural state, in the wild," Dani said.

"Were you ever scared?" Janis asked.

"Not really," Dani replied. He explained that the tour guide was careful not to put anyone at risk.

Dani: It was the best holiday I ever had!

- In the space below, write your own scripted dialogue between Jacques and the safari guide.

Extension Read your dialogue out loud to check how it sounds.

Animal vocabulary

In English, there are a lot of specific names for male, female and young animals.

- Sort the male, female and young animals into the columns below.

	Male	Female	Young
stag, fawn, doe	stag	fawn	doe
cow, calf, bull			
cock, hen, chick			
duckling, duck, drake			
fox, cub, vixen			
gander, gosling, goose			
cub, lion, lioness			
ram, lamb, ewe			
mare, stallion, foal			

- Match the animal with the type of home they live in.

badger		lodge		fox		warren
beaver		hive		otter		earth
bee		sett		rabbit		holt
bird		eyrie		squirrel		den
eagle		nest		lion		drey

- Now find the collective term for a group of the same kind of animals.

a brood		of cattle		a plague		of fish
a herd		of wolves		a school		of insects
a flock		of chickens		a swarm		of monkeys
a litter		of birds		a troop		of lions
a pack		of puppies		a pride		of bees

Producing a comic strip

- Write a factual comic strip about a domestic or farm animal that you are familiar with below. Think carefully about the script and the visual information that will appear in each frame. There are nine frames in the template, but you don't have to use all of them.

1.	2.	3.
4.	5.	6.
7.	8.	9.

Extension Make sure you have included a caption for each frame and added colour to the illustrations.

Negative prefixes

Negative forms of words can be made in English by adding a prefix to the beginning of the word. For example, the word 'unbearable' in 'Jenny's secret' (pages 106–107 of your Student Book) is made by adding the prefix *un-* to the word 'bearable'.

- Several different prefixes can be used to turn words into a negative form. Rewrite each of the words below with the correct negative prefix, taken from the list. You will need to use most of the prefixes more than once.

dis-, il-, im-, in-, ir-, un-					
possible	impossible	ability		known	
direct		perfect		tasteful	
literate		expected		done	
responsible		legal		honest	

Possessives

- Add an apostrophe to show possession to the underlined noun in each of the sentences below. Then write whether they are singular or plural.

Children's books contain lots of pictures.	plural
Mr Greens English lessons were always exciting.	
My mums brothers took her out for dinner to celebrate her promotion.	
The tables were covered in every students books.	
How did the discovery of the seals resting place affect Jenny?	
A tigers stripes help to camouflage it in the wild.	
The horses tails were different shades of brown.	
The childrens toys are kept in a toy box.	

Extension Highlight or circle each of the different prefixes in a different colour. Think of more examples for each prefix.

Vocabulary about the Siberian tiger

The vocabulary below is about the threat to the Siberian tiger caused by humans.

- Fill in the gaps in these extracts from pages 108–109 of your Student Book.

centuries, dying, endangered, extinct, habitat, illegal, reduced, undisturbed, unemployment, uninhabited

Around Vladivostok are _______________ forests known as *taiga*. For many _______________ the forests have provided a _______________ for Siberian tigers where they can live and feed _______________ by human beings. However, Siberian tigers now seem likely to become _______________ which means they may completely die out and become _______________. _______________ is very high in the area and many people have turned to poaching and hunting. These activities are _______________. Although patrols have _______________ the numbers of killings, tigers are still _______________.

Writing a letter

- Write a letter warning a friend about how tigers can be dangerous to people, using the information about tigers you remember from Unit 7 of your Student Book and/or your own research.

Dear

Determiners

Determiners are used to make clear how many or which person or thing a noun refers to. They come before the noun.

- The nouns below are all found in the text of 'The Man-eating Tiger' on pages 111–112 of your Student Book. Add a suitable determiner in each case.

_an_ old man	________ young man	________ distance
________ army	________ days' leave	________ leaves
________ man	________ villagers	________ surrounding forest
________ months	________ cattle track	________ one
________ only son	________ women	________ houses

The most commonly used determiners are articles: 'the', 'a' and 'an'. Other kinds of determiners you will find are: possessives, demonstratives and quantifiers.

- Take the determiners you used in the activity above that were not articles, and place them into the following columns. Some examples are shown for you.

Possessive	Demonstrative	Number/quantifier
their, our	this, these	three, more

- Use some of the determiners from the table above in sentences of your own.

Possessive	His homework was not handed in on time.
Possessive	
Demonstrative	
Number/quantifier	
Number/quantifier	

Extension Make a list of as many indefinite determiners as you can.

8 Living together

In this unit, you will practise direct speech, modal verbs, using the imperative, rhyme schemes and homophones.

Verbs for motivation You will need SB p116

- The verbs below are used in the text 'Can we build artificial islands?' on page 116 of your Student Book. Include each of them in a sentence that shows you understand their meaning.

to have experience with	
to inspire	
to require	
to oppose	

- Write a brief summary of the information in each of the five paragraphs in the text 'Can we build artificial islands?'.

Paragraph 1	
Paragraph 2	
Paragraph 3	
Paragraph 4	
Paragraph 5	

Extension Have you used mostly simple or multi-clause sentences in your summary? Explain why.

Vocabulary for describing direct speech

There are many other words that can be used to describe direct speech apart from 'said'. In the following example, the verb 'sighed' is a more descriptive word than 'said'.

Example: "I'm going to be late again," sighed the businessman.

● Choose a more descriptive word from the list below to fill in the 'speech word' in each sentence.

asked, begged, commanded, complained, cried, insisted, joked, mumbled, sobbed, whispered, yelled

"Get out of the way," the cyclist ___yelled___, "my brakes have failed!"

"I fell down and cut my knee!" _____________ the little boy.

"Have you seen my car keys?" she _____________, when she couldn't find them in her purse.

"Shh! I think they might be able to hear us," the boy _____________ softly.

She _____________ the policeman, "Please let me off, just this once."

"Come here, right now!" _____________ the teacher.

The clown laughed and _____________, "So I got out of bed to tuck my feet back in."

"I want a refund. This bucket I bought has got a hole in it," the boy _____________.

"You must get up early tomorrow, if you want to come with us," _____________ her mother.

Unsure of what to say, he _____________, "Mmm, yes, I think that's, erm, right."

"I can't take it anymore. Just go!" she _____________.

Writing a monologue | You will need SB pp118–119

● Take one of the comments you wrote for the five images with speech bubbles on pages 118–119 of your Student Book, and write an extended monologue for that person in this speech bubble. The character should go into more detail about his or her thoughts and feelings.

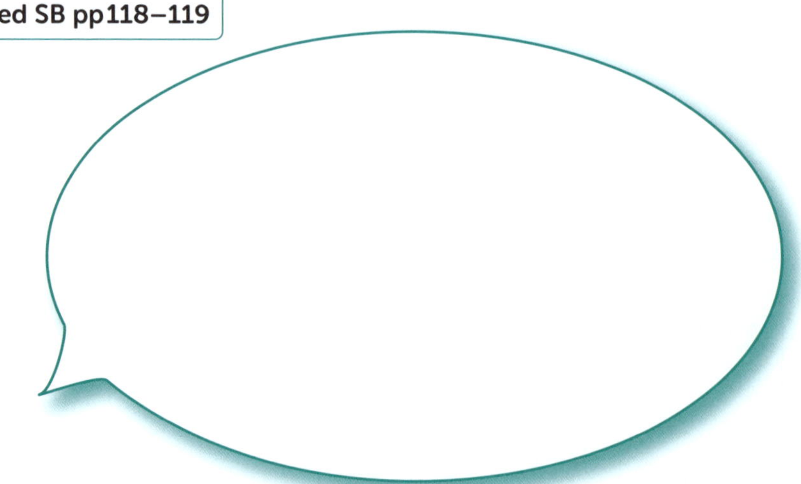

Extension Write five direct speech examples using unique and descriptive 'speech words'.

Modal verbs

Modal verbs are used to express a particular attitude towards something, or the possibility or likelihood of an action or event taking place.

- Add the modal verbs to the sentences below from 'The Red Rooster' text on pages 120–121 of your Student Book.

can't, won't, will

> "It _______________ be helped," the younger brother said to his wife.
>
> "You _______________ get better," the medicine man said, "unless you eat the flesh of a big rooster with fine red feathers."
>
> "You _______________ be cursed and your feathers _______________ grow until he has forgiven you."

- Add any suitable modal verb to the sentences below from the list provided.

~~***can***~~***, can't, could, couldn't, may, might, might not, must, mustn't, shall, should, will, would, wouldn't, ought to***

> I went to listen to them and they ______*can*______ play really well.
>
> He said he _______________ mend it, once the spare part has arrived.
>
> Paula _______________ tell him if she doesn't want to see him anymore.
>
> _______________ I leave ten minutes early today, Mrs Hunter?
>
> The coach revealed he _______________ switch tactics in the second half.
>
> "Cinderella _______________ go to the ball," said the fairy godmother.
>
> _______________ I put that ugly hat on?
>
> I _______________ work early and we could go to the gym.
>
> We _______________ tidy up this mess!
>
> No matter how hard they tried, they _______________ open the door.
>
> If it stops raining, we _______________ go outside.

Extension Write a one-paragraph account of your day at school today. Use a range of modal verbs and simple and multi-clause sentences in your writing.

Using imperative or command verbs

In the story 'The Red Rooster' on pages 120–121 of your Student Book, the author creates dramatic emphasis with the use of imperative or command verbs.

- Fill in the missing verb stem using one of the following examples of the imperative from 'The Red Rooster'.

forgive, go, help, hurry, invite, let us (let's), make, slaughter

> "Then _________________ and ask my brother to give it to me," the older brother moaned.
>
> "And _________________ up. I feel so ill I'm sure I'm about to die."
>
> "_________________ one of our animals," he said to his wife. "_________________ a feast.
> _________________ my friends. _________________ celebrate my recovery."
>
> "_________________!" he shouted. "What's happening to me? I'm growing feathers!"
>
> "Brother, _________________ me," he said.

Strong language

The use of strong language emphasizes the emotional tension between the two brothers in the story 'The Red Rooster'.

- Insert the missing verbs, prepositions and adverbials into the gaps in the sentences below.

after all, but, forgive, greedy, horrid, never, of course, only, selfish, still, ugly, without

> The rich brother sometimes gave feasts for his friends, but he _________________ invited his brother.
>
> "Ah well," the younger brother said. "He is _________________ my brother, after all."
>
> "No, _________________ your brother has," said his wife. "That _________________ thing! It wakes me up every morning with its _________________ crowing."
>
> "Husband," said his younger brother's wife. "That rooster is the _________________ thing we have."
>
> "Brother, _________________ me," he said. "I've been _________________ and _________________, and I took all you have _________________ a word of thanks."
>
> "_________________ I forgive you," he said, "for we are brothers, _________________."

Rhyme schemes

Many poems use rhyme at the ends of lines to create certain effects. The poem 'I'd like to squeeze' (page 123 of your Student Book) does this towards the end, when 'square' and 'share' are used to create an alternate rhyme.

Rhyme schemes use letters to indicate which lines rhyme in a poem, as shown below in the poem 'Daffodils' by William Wordsworth.

> **Tip**
>
> A daffodil is a type of yellow flower that is native to northern Europe.

Daffodils	
I wandered lonely as a <u>cloud</u>	A
That floats on high o'er vales and <u>hills</u>,	B
When all at once I saw a <u>crowd</u>,	A
A host, of golden <u>daffodils</u>;	B
Beside the lake, beneath the <u>trees</u>,	C
Fluttering and dancing in the <u>breeze</u>.	C
WILLIAM WORDSWORTH	

- Complete these poems with your own lines to fit the given rhyme schemes.

Autumn is my favourite season,	A	In summertime I like to play	A
It has the freshest, sweetest air,	B	Out in the fields, under the sun	B
	A		B
	B		A

Rhyming vocabulary

- Match the pairs of rhyming words below. Beware – words that sound the same do not always have the same spellings!

share		died	rhyme		wink	
enough		flair	blood		whole	
pride		verse	think		time	
untrue		stuff	roll		cry	
worse		through	sigh		mud	

Extension Find other pairs of words that have the same rhyming sound but are spelled differently.

Robinson Crusoe vocabulary

- Fill in the gaps in the extract with the correct words from the list below.

bread, crop, damage, effect, fowl, glad, gun, harvested, hung, island,
marvellous, neither, realized, relieved, ruin, starve, supply

But then my crop was under threat of ___________ once more when I found flocks of ___________ pecking at the seeds. I immediately shot at them, for I always had my ___________ with me, but more birds returned. I ___________ that they would destroy all my hopes and I would ___________. I examined the ___________ and found that if I could save what was left of my ___________ all was not lost.

I killed three of the birds and ___________ their bodies from the trees. The ___________ was ___________. So long as my scarecrows hung there, the fowls came ___________ to my crops again, nor even to my part of the ___________. This I was very ___________ of, and at about the end of December, I ___________ my crop. I was very ___________, and I now believed I would be able to ___________ myself with ___________.

Point of view

- Rewrite the first paragraph of the extract from *Robinson Crusoe* on page 125 of your Student Book from the point of view of a narrator.

The ground I had dug up for my crop of barley was not large, for I only had a small amount of seed. My hopes of gathering seed from my first crop had been destroyed. I had planted my first crop in the dry season and it had failed. I was pleased to see my new crop growing well, but then I saw that I was in danger of losing it. Wild goats were devouring it. They were eating the green shoots as soon as they pushed through the earth.

The ground he had dug up for his crop ...

Extension What changes would you have to make to rewrite the paragraph in the second person?

Robinson Crusoe context clues

The extracts below are taken from the original text of *Robinson Crusoe*, written by
Daniel Defoe in 1719. The more unfamiliar words have been underlined.

- Read the extracts and match the underlined words with their definitions.

Finding my first seed did not grow, which I easily imagined was by the drought, I sought for a <u>moister</u> piece of ground to make another trial in …
and this having the rainy months of March and April to water it, sprung up very pleasantly, and <u>yielded</u> a very good crop …
I had but a small quantity at last, my whole crop not amounting to above half a <u>peck</u> of each kind …
But by this <u>experiment</u> I was made master of my business, and knew exactly when the proper season was to sow …

moister	produced fruits or crops through natural growth
yielded	practice, attempt or test
peck	wetter
experiment	old-fashioned measure of about nine litres

Homophones

The words 'their' and 'there' are homophones. They have the same or similar sound,
but a different meaning and spelling.

- Complete the sentences by placing each homophone in the correct place.

higher / hire	He was disappointed to find a __________ charge to __________ the car.
there / their	I was __________ on the day when they won __________ first match.
hour / our	All of __________ rates are priced by the __________.
right / write	You must make sure you __________ the __________ number on the slip.
new / knew	She __________ all along the __________ pupil would get the best mark.

Extension Make a list of as many other homophones as you can think of.

In this unit, you will practise prefixes, multi-clause sentences, prepositions, verb phrases, punctuation and foreign vocabulary.

Using prefixes to express the opposite

The American anthropologist Margaret Mead studied how alike and how unalike people around the world are (you read about this on page 130 of your Student Book).

- Look at the table below. Add a prefix to the words that express similarities to make them into words that express differences.

Words that express similarities	Words that express differences
alike	unalike
similar	
equivalent	
agree	
balanced	
equal	

Multi-clause sentences

The multi-clause sentences below are from 'The Obvious Elephant' on page 132 of your Student Book.

- Match the first and second halves of each sentence, by writing the letter in the boxes provided.

1	G	One day long ago	A	and prodded it with sticks.
2		They made him a necklace of flowers for his huge neck	B	the Professor came along.
3		And when they knew what he was,	C	and went back indoors.
4		The Professor went to his library	D	or how it got there.
5		The villagers looked after the elephant	E	as they, too, prodded it with sticks.
6		At that moment,	F	and found out.
7		The children ran around excitedly,	G	the people of a village woke to find a huge, grey animal.
8		The grown-ups laughed	H	and gave him a name.
9		Some villagers were afraid of the strange monster	I	they made him welcome.
10		No one knew what it was	J	and they lived together happily ever after.

Extension Identify the different parts and clause types of the sentences above.

More prepositions

The following exercise uses extracts from the fable 'The Obvious Elephant' on page 132 of your Student Book.

- Fill in the gaps from the list of prepositions provided below.

after (×2), along, at, for, from, in, of (×2), on, out, round, to, with

One day long ago, the people _______________ a village woke _______________ find a huge, grey animal _______________ the middle _______________ their field. No one knew what it was or how it had got there. The children ran _______________ it excitedly, and prodded it _______________ sticks. _______________ that moment, the Professor came _______________. "I will find _______________ what this animal is," he said. "It's an elephant!" he told the villagers.

They made the elephant a necklace _______________ flowers _______________ his huge neck and gave him a name. _______________ then _______________ the villagers looked _______________ the elephant and they lived happily ever _______________.

You will notice that prepositions often follow a verb and connect it to the noun phrase that comes afterwards.

- Write a sentence of your own using each of the prepositions below.

by	All I want is to live by the sea.	for	
in		at	
from		like	
after		with	
down		as	
but		near	

Extension Write out a list of all the prepositions you know.

Anthropomorphism

Anthropomorphism means giving human characteristics to things that are not human, such as describing an animal driving a car.

- State which of the sentences below are examples of anthropomorphism.

The grown-ups laughed as they too prodded the poor animal.	No
The man and the lion continued to argue.	
The villagers made the elephant a necklace of flowers.	
The lion boasted that he was stronger and braver than a man.	
"Wait a moment, wait a moment," said the lion.	

- Give an example of anthropomorphism of your own.

Summarizing a fable You will need SB p133

- Answer the questions below to summarize the fable you read about the lion by Aesop on page 133 of your Student Book.

What was the problem?
Do you think it was resolved? Explain your answer.
Who were the characters?
What does the ending mean?

Fiction genres

- Match each of the fiction types below with its features.

Genre
romance
science fiction
contemporary
historical
fantasy
mystery
action
fables
horror

Features
danger, a narrow escape
heartache involved
clues to solve
advanced technology
a moral to be learned
real-life setting
scary, events that shock
events from the past
extraordinary creatures

- Think back to some of the story extracts you have read in your Student Book. What genre would you say each of the following stories is?

Unit 1: 'The river gypsies' _______________________________

Unit 1: 'Fresh water to drink' _______________________________

Unit 3: 'Something in the Air' _______________________________

Unit 4: 'Shauzia's dream' _______________________________

Unit 5: 'Ningnong's great day' _______________________________

Unit 6: 'The Dinner that Cooked Itself' _______________________________

Unit 8: 'The Red Rooster' _______________________________

Unit 8: 'My first harvest' _______________________________

Unit 8: 'Toro! Toro!' _______________________________

Unit 9: 'The Obvious Elephant' _______________________________

Verb phrases

Verb phrases have been used in both fables on pages 132 and 133 of your Student Book to give additional information about the verb.

- Match each of the verb phrases below with a single-verb synonym.

to come along
to run around
to go back
to find out
to look after
to walk along

to guard
to discover
to stroll
to accompany
to encircle
to return

- Choose four of the verb phrases from the list above and use them in some sentences of your own.

Introductory phrases

It is useful when writing compositions to come up with some good introductory phrases to get you started, such as, 'One day long ago' or 'There was once a man'.

- Complete these sentences.

When I was only five years old …
The day started off as normal but …
I thought it was going to be a normal day at school …
I should have expected there to be a problem when …
The first time I saw …

- Write your own sample introductory phrases.

Punctuation

- The text below is from the interview with AJ the actor on page 140 of your Student Book. Rewrite it, adding all the missing punctuation. Use as full a range of punctuation as you need, and remember to add upper-case letters where needed.

<table>
<tr><td align="center">, . ? ! ' '</td></tr>
</table>

hi AJ thanks for saying youll answer a few questions what made you want to become an actor I asked

oh wow well when I was younger I fancied the fame and money I wasnt very academic I was also big into movies and liked to copy the characters who were in my favourite films he replied

what do you like most about being an actor I asked

He replied I like looking through the eyes of someone else and walking in their shoes also its great to act badly and have no repercussions

Extension Find out what the difference is between em dashes, commas and brackets when adding extra information.

Borrowed words

- Match each word borrowed from another language below with its equivalent.

trek	boat	cookie	disguise
wigwam	journey	roster	dog
dinghy	song	camouflage	biscuit
carol	corn	geyser	list
maize	tent	corgi	fountain

More borrowed words

- Here are examples of words that English has borrowed from other languages. Find out what language they have come from, explain their meaning, and then show how each can be used in a sentence.

Word	Original language	Meaning	Sentence
bungalow	Hindi and Urdu		
candy			
carte blanche			
delicatessen			
en masse			
faux pas			
prima donna			
rendezvous			
shampoo			
status quo			

10 Rubbish

In this unit, you will practise synonyms and look at playscripts, symbolism, and formal and informal language.

Synonyms

Synonyms are often used to avoid repeating the same word, for example, in the article about discarded food on page 147 of your Student Book, food waste is described as 'rejected', 'saved' and 'rescued'.

- Match the pairs of synonyms in the lists below.

customers
decaying
food waste
surplus
well-known
thrown out
waste disposal site

leftovers
discarded
prominent
landfill
rotten
excess
consumers

- Choose one from each of the pairs of synonyms and use it in a sentence to show its meaning.

A lot of people cook too much food which is then <u>thrown out</u> and wasted.

Extension Now rewrite some of your sentences above using new and different synonyms for any and all the words.

Comparing texts

- Read the two extracts below from your Student Book about recycling unwanted items (on pages 155–156 and pages 160–161).

The junk orchestra	**What is a Repair Café?**
An oil drum was a good body for a cello; a bent kitchen fork for a violin tailpiece. The first few scratchy instruments were given to local kids for whom a new violin might cost a month of their parents' wages. Chávez began to train his ensemble. "This is not a place where someone can have a violin. A violin is worth more than a house here. A violin made out of trash is worth nothing, so it will not be sold or stolen," he says.	Visitors bring their broken items from home. Together with the specialists they start making their repairs in the Repair Café. It's an ongoing learning process. If you have nothing to repair, you can enjoy a cup of tea or coffee. Or you can lend a hand with someone else's repair job. You can also get inspired at the reading table – by leafing through books on repairs and DIY.

- Fill in the Venn diagram below, writing the differences between the two extracts in the outer parts of the circle and similarities where the circles overlap.

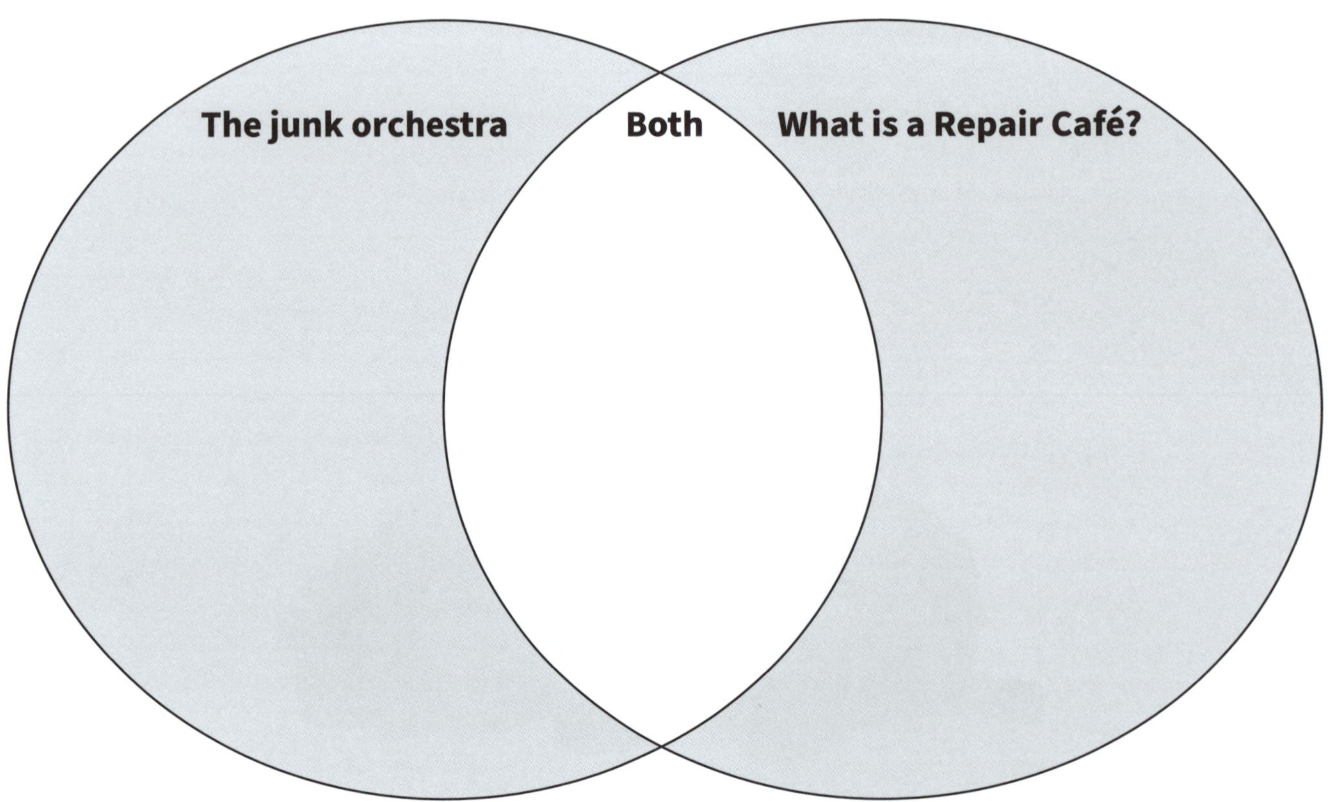

Writing a playscript

Here is an extract from the story *Trash* on pages 157–158 of your Student Book.

- Rewrite it as a conversation between Raphael and Gardo in the form of a playscript. Don't forget to include stage directions.

It fell into my hand: a small leather bag, zipped up tight and covered in coffee-grounds. Unzipping it, I found a wallet. Next to that, a folded-up map – and inside the map, a key. Gardo came right over, and we squatted there together, up on the hill. My fingers were trembling, because the wallet was fat. There were eleven hundred pesos inside, and that – let me tell you – is good money. A chicken costs one-eighty . . . One hour in the video hall, twenty-five. I sat there laughing . . . Gardo was punching me, and I don't mind telling you, we almost danced. I gave him five hundred, which was fair because I was the one who found it. Six hundred left for me.

Raphael	Gardo! Come here! Look what just fell into my hand! *(Gardo walks over.)*
Gardo	What is it?

Extension Make a list of the features of a playscript. Check there aren't any that you have left out in the playscript you have written.

Symbolism

Writers use words as symbols to add extra meaning to their writing that is beyond the literal meaning of the word. They might use objects, people or colours to stand for a hidden or more complicated idea.

- Match the symbols below with their common connotation or implied meaning.

Symbol	Connotation
white snow	hope and new beginnings
wedding ring	peace
season of spring	power
white dove	evil and sinister
wild-fire	purity and decency
thick fog	friendship
hissing snake	commitment to someone or something
speeding train	destruction and lack of control
a heart	shows someone is lost
a handshake	love and kindness

- Colours are often used as symbols. Explain what the following colours mean to you.

Colour	Connotation
red	love, anger
green	
orange	
white	
black	
blue	

Extension Create simple emojis for some of the words above to symbolize their meaning, such as a drawing of a white dove.

The prefix *re-*

Throughout the unit 'Rubbish', you will encounter words beginning with the prefix *re-*. The prefix *re-* means 'again'.

- Use each of the following words beginning with the prefix *re-* in a sentence that has a connection to any of the topics in Unit 10. Make sure the meaning of the *re-* word is made clear.

reuse, recycle, rebuild, rearrange, rejoin, ~~rearrange~~, redo, reheat, refresh, rethink

1	You should <u>rearrange</u> your rubbish so that it is organized separately into plastics, glass, and paper.
2	
3	
4	
5	
6	
7	
8	
9	
10	

Extension We see symbols around us in everyday life. Three green arrows in a triangle is the symbol that shows something can be recycled. What other symbols can you think of connected to rubbish and waste collection?

Formal and informal language

Formal and informal language have different features: formal language will use complex sentences and Standard English, while informal language uses contracted words, abbreviations and slang, for example.

- Change the following paragraph from informal into formal language.

> I thought I'd call my best mate so we could hang out. He was flat out in bed so I asked 'What's up?' He said he flunked the science test and was so cheesed off that he fell off his bike and messed up his knee. What an idiot! He didn't exactly get tons of sympathy from me. Anyway, I just hope his knee fixes ASAP as I've forked out a lot of cash to see our fave band – they are HUGE. But if he can't come there are a bunch of other guys who'd grab his ticket so it's no big deal.

I decided to telephone my best friend in order for us to arrange to spend time together.

- The following list is written in a formal style. Rewrite the words in informal language using a word or phrase from the list below.

crash, wanna, tight, shades, gonna, sweet, chill, lol, my bad, hang out

Formal	Informal
excellent	*sweet*
in a close relationship	
spend time with	
sunglasses	
relax	
fall asleep	
sorry, I made a mistake	
going to	
want to	
that is amusing	

11 Community

In this unit, you will practise auxiliary verbs, conjunctive adverbs and homographs.

Vocabulary about community

- Place the correct words into each of the sentences below.

citizen, co-operation, group, identity, kinship, membership, neighbourhood, shared interests, society

The people in Stella's ———————— all came from very different backgrounds, but they got on very well.

Fred told his class he saw himself as a ———————— as well as a brother, son and student.

The two villages pooled their resources as they had ———————— in the water-pump project.

The aim of good government is to try to help everyone in ———————— to live a safe, prosperous and healthy life.

Everyone who lived in the street took care to look after their ———————— and keep it safe.

Amjad felt a strong sense of ———————— with his classmates after they had gone on a cricket tour together.

Nothing could have been achieved without the ———————— of the local schools.

Mkwande had a complex ————————: he was born in America, had family in Tanzania, and studied in Germany.

The president gave a speech addressing the entire ———————— of the beach workers' trade union.

Extension Think of other words that are useful in discussions about community.
What kind of words are most useful in a global community?

Adverbs as conjunctions

You often need to link ideas and points together. Sometimes these points will be contrasting ones, and sometimes you will want to link together similar points. Conjunctive adverbs are important words to use in non-fiction writing. For example, 'I ate too much cake and, <u>consequently</u>, I was ill'. There are more conjunctive adverbs listed below.

☐	accordingly	☐	besides	☐	consequently	☐	furthermore
☐	however	☐	likewise	☐	certainly	☐	nevertheless
☐	otherwise	☐	similarly	☐	subsequently	☐	therefore

- Think about the poem 'Finding a Friend' on page 166 of your Student Book. Use the space below to write down your ideas on the importance of friendship. Use as many of the adverbs above to link your ideas as you can. Tick the box next to each adverb that you use.

Homographs

The word 'produce' in Señor Juárez's interview (pages 168–169 of your Student Book) can be used as a noun and a verb. There are quite a few words in English that are spelled the same but have a different meaning, and are pronounced slightly differently. They are called *homographs*.

- Use separate colours to circle each word in the left column to match it with the two possible meanings of the word given in the other two columns by circling them in the same colour.

produce	*(v)* to be opposed	*(adj)* extremely small
conflict	*(n)* a period of 60 seconds	*(n)* a product (for example, fruit)
minute	*(v)* to make	*(n)* something thrown away
present	*(v)* to propel with oars	*(n)* an argument
reject	*(v)* to show	*(n)* fighting or war
row	*(v)* to rip	*(n)* a drop of water shed by an eye
tear	*(v)* to get rid of	*(n)* a gift

Vocabulary for preparing food

- Match the following verbs with their correct definition.

to bake	to mix in smoothly
to blend	to strip something of its outer layer
to fry	to whip or mix rapidly with sweeping movements
to grate	to work into a uniform texture by pressing, folding and stretching
to juice	to extract liquid from a vegetable or fruit
to knead	to cook in liquid just below boiling point
to peel	to cook by dry heat, usually in an oven
to purée	to reduce to small particles
to rub	to cook with fat in a shallow pan
to simmer	to make into a cream or liquid
to whisk	to cook with fat in a shallow pan

Recreating *Doctor Dolittle*

Recreate the story of *Doctor Dolittle* (on pages 174–175 of your Student Book) in the two activities below. Try to carry out this exercise from memory.

● Match the two sentence halves together to recreate the full multi-clause sentences.

The Doctor talked to him in crocodile-language	they did not want to go away.
Some of the animals were so sick	if it had never been invented.
But to everyone in the house	and took him into the house.
But when the crocodile saw what a nice house it was	that they had to stay at the Doctor's house for a week.
We'd all be much better off	because she was the oldest.
And often even after they got well	he too wanted to live with the Doctor.
They made Polynesia housekeeper	he was always as gentle as a kitten.

● Fill in the gaps with the verbs and verb phrases that have been taken out.

watch, found, sweeping, used to think, never had, hard to do, got to do, got used to

Of course at first they all _______________ their new jobs very _______________ – all except Chee-Chee, who had hands … But they soon _______________ it; and they _______________ it great fun to _______________ Jip, the dog, _______________ over the floor with a rag tied onto it for a broom. After a little while they _______________ the work so well that the Doctor said that he had _______________ his house kept so tidy or so clean before.

Main and auxiliary verbs

The main verb specifies the action in a phrase. Auxiliary verbs make the meaning of the main verb clearer by describing the timing or likelihood of the action, or an attitude towards it.

- Underline the main verbs in each of these verb phrases taken from the *Doctor Dolittle* extract. Write a sentence of your own using the same main and auxiliary verbs.

can speak	
are sick	
were sick	
could stay	
was asleep	
didn't worry	
ought to do	
can do	
was agreed	

- Use the verbs below to fill in the gaps in this summary about *Doctor Dolittle*.

would, was, must, did, were, wanted

Doctor Dolittle's house _____________ full to the brim with animals. He _____________ allows them to stay when they _____________ well. The crocodile _____________ have been very happy because he chased his keepers away. The animals _____________ to help so they agreed they _____________ clean the house.

Extension Highlight the main verbs and any modal verbs in the extract above.

Writing a letter

- Imagine Doctor Dolittle is your uncle and you are staying with him for the summer. Write a letter to a family member or a friend, telling them about the unusual community you are living in.

The Surgery

Puddleby-on-the-Marsh

West Country

England

29th June 1820

Dear

Extension Make sure that you have used multi-clause sentences, conjunctive adverbs, noun phrases, and verb phrases in your letter.

How can we best work together?

- Think back to the cartoon of the two donkeys working together on page 176 of your Student Book. Write up the story behind the donkey cartoon as a fable. Use the checklist below as you write, to make sure you include the following features.

<table>
<tr><td>☐</td><td>Use anthropomorphism to give the donkeys human characteristics.</td></tr>
<tr><td>☐</td><td>Make use of separate paragraphs.</td></tr>
<tr><td>☐</td><td>Write your dialogue between the donkeys in direct speech.</td></tr>
<tr><td>☐</td><td>Include a moral at the end of your fable.</td></tr>
</table>

Extension Explain how the moral of your story could be applied to a situation that you might come across at home or at school.

⑫ Courage

In this unit, you will practise modal verbs, think about biographies, look at similes, metaphors and hyperbole, and examine news reports and diaries.

Practising modal verbs

You will have found examples of modal verbs in the extract about Iqbal Masih on pages 179–181 of your Student Book. Modal verbs show the likelihood of something happening. They come before the main verb.

- Underline the modal verbs in each of the following sentences.

> If I couldn't eat ice-cream, I might drink iced tea instead.
>
> The film will start at 7.30 but we can't get to the cinema until 7.45.
>
> The sun may shine this afternoon even though the forecast says we should expect some showers.
>
> In spite of the cloud, we ought to see the comet tonight, although we mustn't expect to get a very good view.

Modal verbs also alter the urgency of other verbs. For example, 'Iqbal <u>can</u> work in a carpet-making factory' can change to 'Ibqal <u>must</u> work in a carpet-making factory'.

- Underline the strongest, most urgent modal verb in each list.

can	could	might	shouldn't	couldn't	mustn't
may	must	ought to	can't	won't	oughtn't to

- Change the crossed-out modal verb in the sentences below to another suitable modal verb that makes the action sound more urgent. Use a different modal verb in each sentence.

> You ~~might~~ —————— get put in the cage again if you anger the master.
>
> His friends ~~could~~ —————— bring him food and water.
>
> He ~~should~~ —————— get plenty of rest in order to get better soon.
>
> The children ~~may~~ —————— be braver in future because of Iqbal's actions.

Extension Imagine the ultimate hero. Write about him or her using as many modal verbs as possible (for example, 'She would save everyone from a burning house') to add drama to your writing.

Biographies

A biography is about a person's life but written by someone else, as opposed to an autobiography which is written by someone about their own life.

- Which of these are features of biographical writing?

Feature	Yes/No
Contains dates	
Asks questions	
Has a protagonist and antagonist	
Written in chronological order	
Uses technical language	
Written in first person	
Written in third person	
Important events are recalled	
There is a lesson to be learned	
Contains writer's opinions	
Written in past tense	
Uses persuasive language	
Uses repetition	
Time conjunctions are used	

- Write a short biography about someone you know well, either a family member or a friend you have known for a long time. As it is short, only pick out the most important events. Use the box below to note down the events you want to include. Use a separate piece of paper to write it out in full.

Extension What types of writing do the features in the table above that you said 'No' to belong to?

Practising similes and metaphors

Similes and metaphors compare one thing to another and provide extra detail to help the reader picture the scene. The difference is that a simile states that one thing is *like* or *as something as* another thing ('he is <u>as</u> cheeky <u>as</u> a monkey'), whereas a metaphor states that one thing *is* another thing ('he <u>is</u> a cheeky monkey') and isn't actually true.

- Change the following similes into metaphors. Add extra words if needed.

Simile: He is as cheeky as a monkey.

Metaphor: *He is a cheeky monkey.* ____

Simile: He is like a ray of sunshine in my life.

Metaphor: ____

Simile: When she sings, her voice is like pure nectar.

Metaphor: ____

Simile: He got the audience so excited it was as though he was on fire.

Metaphor: ____

- Change these metaphors into similes. Add extra words if needed.

Metaphor: He is a cheeky monkey.

Simile: *He is as cheeky as a monkey.* ____

Metaphor: It's raining cats and dogs!

Simile: ____

Metaphor: The world is a stage and is full of actors.

Simile: ____

Metaphor: The ground was covered in a thick blanket of snow.

Simile: ____

Hyperbole

Hyperbole is used to add humour and exaggeration to writing, so much so that what is written is not believable. There are examples in the poem 'Being Brave at Night' on page 185 of your Student Book.

- Underline the hyperbole in the following sentences.

> I'll do my homework later; it'll only take me <u>a second</u>.
>
> I've told you a million times that I didn't break the window!
>
> I love my new phone but it cost me an arm and a leg.
>
> My singing is so bad that it'd sink the Titanic.
>
> This movie is as old as the hills and I've seen it thousands of times.

- Explain what the hyperbole in each of these sentences is telling you.

This is taking forever!	Something is taking a long time to do.
My English teacher is older than the dinosaurs.	
I slept like a log last night.	
My mum's given me enough sandwiches to feed an army!	
Our new house cost an arm and a leg.	

- Using the ideas on the left, write your own sentences containing hyperbole.

You are very thirsty.	I'm so thirsty I could drink a whole swimming pool.
There is a bear chasing you.	
Someone is very happy.	
A new, shiny diamond ring.	
A man who shouts loudly.	

Extension Make a note of any hyperbole you, your friends, or your family use regularly.

News reports

● Fill in the diagram below with the features you find in a written news report.

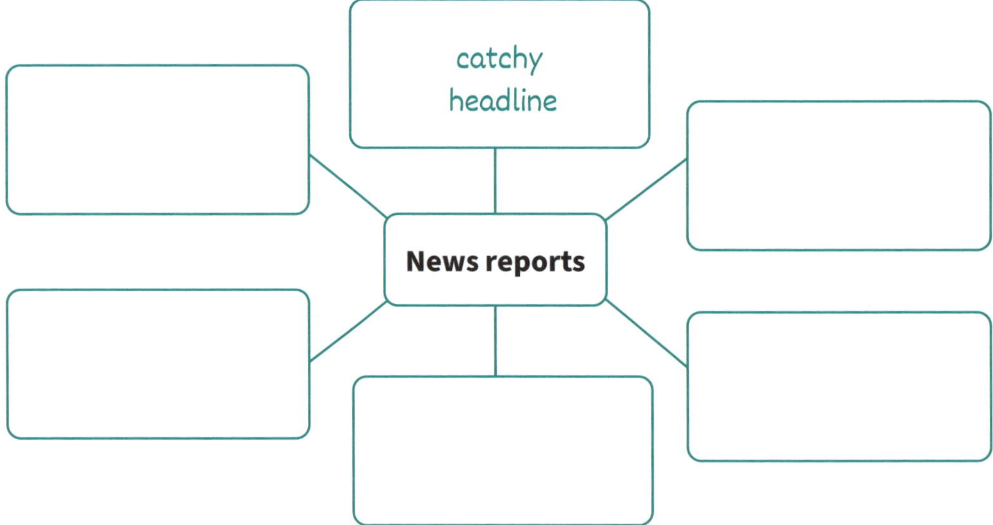

● Imagine you are a radio reporter at the match girls' protest rally in Hyde Park in the extract on pages 187–189 of your Student Book, giving a live report to your listeners. Write an account of what you are saying to them. They need to know what is happening, who is involved, and where, when, and why the protest is taking place. Make your language suitable for your audience and remember, they can only hear your voice and cannot see what you can see.

Well, good afternoon to our listeners. This is _________________ reporting to you from Hyde Park in London. You won't believe what's happening here today.

Extension What features make a spoken news report different to a written one?

Diary entries | You will need SB p191

- Captain Scott's diary contains a lot of language that infers unpleasant events have taken place. Think back to his diary extract on page 191 of your Student Book and write what you think Scott is inferring in the quotes below.

Quote	Inference
Tragedy all along the line.	
… he proposed that we should leave him in his sleeping bag.	
… we knew the end had come.	
He said, "I am just going outside and may be some time."	

- Write a diary entry recounting your day today. It doesn't have to be dramatic or exciting. You may want to comment on what you did, how you felt, the weather, or if you were with friends. Use suitable vocabulary for a personal diary.

Extension Evaluate the diary entry you have just written. How do you rate your use of chatty language, informal style, use of the first person, and the inclusion of interesting vocabulary?

Here are all the cross-curricular words you are learning this year. Highlight any words you don't know and read the definitions. Use this list for reference as you complete the activities on the following pages.

attitude *noun* the way you think about something or react to people
'His positive attitude helped everyone enjoy the trip.'

belief *noun* 1. the feeling that something exists or is true
'The young girl held on to her belief in the kindness of others.'
2. to have belief in someone is to have trust or confidence in them
'The coach needs to have more belief in the abilities of the players.'

bias *noun* an opinion or feeling that strongly favours one side in preference to another
'The university has a bias towards the sciences.'

citizen *noun* a person belonging to a particular city or country
'My mother is now an Australian citizen.'

civilization *noun* 1. a society or culture at a particular time in history
'My brother is studying ancient civilizations.'
2. a developed or organized way of life
'Wow! We are so far from civilization here!'

coincidence *noun* an instance of things happening at the same time by chance
'By coincidence, we both went to the same school.'

concern *noun* something that concerns you or worries you; a responsibility
'There is concern that the giant panda will soon become extinct.'
verb 1. to worry or affect someone
'This does not concern you!'
2. to have as the theme or subject
'The story concerns the discovery of a map.'

considerate *adjective* taking care not to inconvenience or hurt others
'He is always considerate of other people's feelings.'

consult *verb* to go to a person, book, app or other source for information or advice
'I need to consult a dictionary to understand the meaning of this word.'

culture *noun* 1. the customs and traditions of a particular people
'Welcoming strangers is important in their culture.'
2. the appreciation and understanding of literature, art, music, and other creative achievements
'My grandfather is a person of great culture.'

deceive *verb* to make someone believe something that is not true
'His gentle, kind words did not deceive me – I knew he was lying.'

discriminate *verb* to treat people differently or unfairly, for example because of their race, gender, age, or religion
'You should not discriminate against minorities.'

elaborate *adjective* having many parts or details
'She had prepared a very elaborate meal.'
verb to explain or work out a plan or design in detail
'He said he was resigning from his job but did not elaborate.'

emotional *adjective* having strong feelings in your mind, such as love, anger, or hate
'My father made an emotional speech at the wedding.'

emphasize *verb* to place special importance on something
'He banged his fist on the table to emphasize his point.'

ethical *adjective* morally right; honourable
'The use of animals in scientific tests raises some difficult ethical questions.'

hazard *noun* a danger or risk
'Polluted water sources are a hazard to wildlife.'

humane *adjective* showing kindness and a wish to cause as little suffering as possible
'Animals are now raised in more humane conditions.'

jeopardy *noun* danger of harm or failure
'The future of the school is in jeopardy.'

mislead *verb* to give somebody a wrong idea or impression deliberately
'I won't mislead you – learning a new language is not easy!'

narration *noun* telling a story or giving an account of something
'A famous actor did the narration for this documentary.'

nostalgic *adjective* feeling pleasure, mixed with sadness, when you remember happy
times in the past
'I get very nostalgic when I go back to my hometown.'

original *adjective* 1. existing from the start; earliest
'Who was the original owner of this house?'
2. new in design; not a copy
'The thieves replaced the original painting with a copy.'

persuade *verb* to make someone believe or agree to do something
'Please try and persuade her to come to the party.'

prediction *noun* saying what will happen in the future
'My prediction that we would win the match was right'

principle *noun* 1. a general truth, belief, or rule
'He taught us the basic principles of making bread.'
2. a rule of conduct based on what a person believes is right
'It is against her principles to wear leather.'

productive *adjective* 1. producing a lot of things
'To turn the deserts into productive land, they built a canal.'
2. producing good results; useful
'My time spent in the library was very productive.'

reflective *adjective* 1. reflecting light, heat, or sound
'On dark nights cyclists should wear reflective clothing.'
2. thoughtful or pensive
'After hearing the sad news, they sat in reflective silence.'

sentimental *adjective* showing or arousing tenderness or romantic feeling or foolish
emotion
'This watch belonged to my grandfather so it has great sentimental value.'

tolerant *adjective* willing to accept or tolerate other people's behaviour and opinions even if you do not agree with them
'I am glad that my parents are tolerant of my fashion choices.'

traditional *adjective* to do with the passing down of beliefs or customs from one generation to another
'This village has its own traditional dress, food and handicrafts.'

view *noun* 1. what can be seen from one place, especially a beautiful or interesting scene
'From our hotel room we had an incredible view of the beach.'
2. an opinion
'He tried to explain his views on the matter.'
verb 1. to look at something
'We took time to view the lake.'
2. to consider or regard someone or something in a particular way
'She viewed him with deep suspicion.'

worthy *adjective* deserving respect or support
'The team played well and were worthy winners.'

Practice

1 Match the underlined words in each sentence to the word with the same meaning.

Looking at the photos from my childhood made me feel quite <u>emotional</u>.	tolerant
The polluted river is a <u>danger</u> to the surrounding wildlife.	nostalgic
We saw several <u>real</u> paintings by Monet when we visited the museum in Paris.	reflective
I was in a <u>thoughtful</u> mood as I walked back home after school.	hazard
There are times when I make my parents angry, but they are usually very <u>patient</u>.	original

2 Fill in the missing words in each sentence with one of the words below.

deceive, mislead, view, jeopardy, coincidence, narration

a His friendly manner did not _____________________ us for long – we soon found out that he was the thief!

b Bumping into my schoolteacher while we were on our family holiday was a remarkable _____________________.

c The lives of thousands of birds are in _____________________ as a result of the oil spillage.

d The _____________________ from the roof was incredible. We could see the mountains and the ocean!

e I am not going to _____________________ you. Being a teacher can be a difficult job!

f Who did the _____________________ for this programme? The voice sounds very familiar to me.

3 Write sentences of your own using each of the words below.

worthy, considerate, productive, humane, traditional, emotional

a ____

b ____

c ____

d ____

e ____

f ____

4 Find synonyms (words with the same meaning) and antonyms (words with the opposite meaning) of the words in the grid and add them to the appropriate column. Try to think of as many of each as you can.

	Synonyms	Antonyms
attitude	opinion	fact
citizen		
principle		
emphasize		
discriminate		
culture		

5 How many new words can you make from these words? You can add or remove letters, find words within words, and add prefixes or suffixes. Then write sentences using the new words.

consult	
ethical	
sentimental	
belief	
bias	
elaborate	

6 Fill in the speech bubbles using one of the words from the box in each bubble. You can change the form of the word to make it fit, for example, "I am so excited about the game tonight. I just can't <u>predict</u> the result!" You can make the speech bubbles as funny or unusual as you like. Work with a partner and use your imagination. Use a dictionary or the internet to help with spelling.

civilization   prediction   persuade

7 Now it's time to get really creative!

If you are working with a partner:

- Choose **six** words from the list on pages 84–86 that you think are the most useful.
- Take turns to explain a word to your partner, describing it, but WITHOUT SAYING THE WORD.

If you are working alone:

- Choose **six** words from the list on pages 84–86 that you think are the most useful.
- Write a story of your choice using the six words. You can add prefixes and suffixes to the words as well.
- The images below are to help give you ideas for your story.

8 You are going to write a news report on a subject of your choice. In the report, you must include at least **six** cross-curricular words. You can either write them in the box below before you begin, or decide on the words as you write and then add them to the box.

Grammar and language terms

active voice a set of verb forms in which the subject of a verb performs the action

'The dog is chasing the cat.'

adverbial a word or phrase which gives more information about a verb or about a clause. An adverbial can be an adverb, a phrase or a subordinate clause.

Adverbials tell you where, when, why, how or how often something is done.

'The dog slept <u>under</u> the table.'

'I <u>usually</u> do my homework before I watch TV.'

'Jack worked <u>very hard</u>.'

'The cat sleeps <u>all day</u>.'

Adverbials sometimes appear at the beginning of a sentence. These are called 'fronted adverbials'. There is usually a comma after a fronted adverbial.

'<u>First thing in the morning</u>, I walk the dog.'

'<u>Next</u>, I have my breakfast.'

Some adverbials link ideas across paragraphs or within paragraphs. These adverbials are often fronted and are usually followed by a comma.

'on the other other hand'; 'in contrast'; 'as a result'; 'secondly'

alliteration occurs when two or more nearby words start with the same sound

'a <u>s</u>low, <u>s</u>ad, <u>s</u>orrowful <u>s</u>ong'

anthropomorphism giving human characteristics, emotions or behaviours to animals, things and gods. Characters like Simba and the other talking lions from *The Lion King*, the Cheshire Cat, the Caterpillar and the White Rabbit from *Alice in Wonderland*, and the gods from Greek mythology are examples of anthropomorphism.

auxiliary verbs these are used with main verbs to indicate continuous actions or to form different tenses. 'Be' and 'have' are auxiliary verbs.

'I <u>am</u> eating.'

'It <u>has</u> rained all night.'

The auxiliary verb 'do' is used in negative statements, questions and commands.

'I <u>do</u> not want any more chocolate.'

'<u>Do</u> you want some?'

'<u>Do</u> sit still!'

clause a group of words that contains a subject and a verb. Every full sentence contains at least one main clause.

'I ran.' (In this clause, 'I' is the subject and 'ran' is the verb.)

Multi-clause sentences contain one or more subordinate clauses. A subordinate clause does not make sense on its own and relies on the main clause.

'<u>When I had finished reading it</u>, I returned the book to the library.' (In this sentence, the clause 'When I had finished reading it' is a subordinate clause, which depends on the main clause, 'I returned the book to the library', to make sense.)

comparative comparative adjectives are used when two things are being compared

'Morning break is only fifteen minutes, but the lunch break is <u>longer</u>.'

'My brother finds maths <u>more difficult</u> than English.'

conditional (relating to) a sentence in which one part expresses something which depends on the other part. Conditional sentences often begin 'if' or 'unless'.

'If I win this race, I will get a prize.'

conjugation the way a verb conjugates. To conjugate a verb means to give all the different forms of a verb according to tense and person.

conjunction a word used to link words or clauses within a sentence

'and'; 'but'; 'so'; 'until'; 'when'; 'as'

'He was running <u>when</u> he went to the shops.'

conjunctive adverb a type of adverb that joins two clauses in a sentence, creating a link between them. Conjunctive adverbs can also show the cause and effect of an action.

'accordingly'; 'also'; 'besides'; 'consequently'; 'finally'; 'however'; 'indeed'; 'instead'

contraction when an apostrophe is used to show that letters have been removed from a word

'didn't' (for 'did not'); 'it's' (for 'it is')

determiner a word like 'a', 'the', 'some', 'any', 'my', 'each', 'every', 'either', and 'no' which is used before a noun, or at the start of a noun phrase. Determiners tell you which one, how many or how much.

'<u>The</u> girls enjoyed <u>the</u> music.'

'There is <u>a</u> bird on <u>the</u> branch.'

'<u>Each</u> box contained 20 books.'

dialogue an oral or written conversation

direct speech when speech marks are used to show that someone is speaking

"Can I talk to you please?" asked Sam.

expanded noun phrase a noun phrase that has a noun as its head, or key word: 'ball' (noun); 'the ball' (noun phrase). Expanded noun phrases add more detail to the noun by adding one or more adjectives, or by saying where the noun is.

'the red pencil on the floor by the desk'

figurative language figurative language uses words for the effects they create, rather than their literal meanings. It often produces vivid images and sounds in the mind of the reader or listener. The most common types of figurative language are: simile, metaphor, personification, hyperbole and onomatopoeia.

'This homework will take forever!' (hyperbole)

'My hands are as cold as ice.' (simile)

'Her eyes blazed with anger.' (metaphor)

genre a type of writing. Poetry, fantasy and non-fiction are examples of different genres.

homograph homographs are words that are spelled the same way but not necessarily pronounced the same way and have different meanings and origins

Spelled the same way but pronounced differently:
'A <u>tear</u> rolled down Sasha's cheek.'
'<u>Tear</u> the form off and send it to the address below.'
Spelled and pronounced the same:
'The head teacher <u>rose</u> from her seat.'

'The ball landed in the <u>rose</u> bushes.'

homophone one of two or more words that sound the same but have different meanings. They may have the same or different spellings.

'right' and 'write'; 'meat' and 'meet'

idiom a colourful expression that cannot be understood from the meaning of its separate words

'It's raining cats and dogs.' (This means that it is raining very hard.)

imperative the form of the verb used to make commands

'<u>Go</u> away!'

indirect speech speech that has been reported but not in the exact words or in quotation marks; also called **reported speech**

irregular verb any verb that does not follow the expected pattern of conjugation in some way. In English, this is usually by not adding *-ed* or *-d* to its past tense form.

'go' (went); 'is' (was); 'do' (did); 'eat' (ate); 'get' (got); 'have' (had); 'make' (made)

main verb the most important verb in the sentence. It describes the action or state of the subject of the sentence.

'The children <u>climbed</u> the tree.'

'We <u>ate</u> a large bar of chocolate during the film.'

metaphor a way of speaking or writing in which one thing is said to be something else. This way of speaking or writing is called a figure of speech.

'Thanks for your help. <u>You are a star</u>!'

modal verb modal verbs are used with a verb to show what is possible, or necessary, or what is going to happen (including 'could', 'should', 'must', 'shall', 'may', 'might', 'will' and 'would')

'I <u>should</u> go for a walk.'

'I <u>can</u> lend you my textbook if you need it.'

multi-clause sentence a sentence that consists of more than one clause

'The girl ran to her mother because she was afraid of the dog.'

noun phrase a small group of words containing a noun or pronoun and one or more modifiers

'the little boy'; 'my green sports bag'

passive voice verb forms in which the subject of the sentence is the person or thing affected by the verb

'A window <u>was broken</u>.'

personification the technique of giving human qualities to things that are not human, such as an animal, concept or inanimate object

'The sun beamed happily while the kittens played hide-and-seek, and life danced by.'

phrase a small group of words that forms part of a clause. Phrases do not make sense on their own.

'The man lives <u>on the hill</u>.'

possessive determiners these are used with a noun to show who or what it belongs to or is related to, for example 'my', 'your', 'his', 'her', 'its', 'our', and 'their'

'Is it okay to wear <u>my</u> trainers?'

possessive pronouns these tell you who owns the thing you are talking about or who is involved in the process or action. Possessive pronouns are used instead of the noun, for example 'mine', 'yours', 'his', 'hers', 'ours' and 'theirs'.

'Is that school jumper <u>mine</u> or <u>yours</u>?'

prefix a word or syllable placed at the beginning of a word to modify its meaning. For example, in the word 'misunderstand', the prefix *mis-* makes the word 'understand' mean 'not understand correctly'. In the word 'unhappy', the prefix *un-* makes the word 'happy' mean 'not happy'.

preposition a word that indicates place ('on', 'in'), direction ('over', 'beyond'), or time ('during', 'on'), among others

'I put the book <u>in</u> the drawer.'

'I read my book <u>during</u> lunch.'

relative clause a type of subordinate clause introduced using the relative pronouns 'that', 'which', 'who', 'whom', and 'whose'

'The film <u>that we watched yesterday</u> was very exciting.'

reported speech when you report someone's words in a changed form

"I am at home." *(direct speech)* becomes 'She said that she was at home.' *(reported speech)*

simile a figure of speech in which two things are compared using the linking words 'like' or 'as'

'In battle, he was <u>as brave as a lion</u>.'

'He behaves <u>like a brave lion</u>.'

simple present tense used when an action is happening at the present moment, or when it happens regularly. Depending on the person, the simple present tense is formed by using the root form of the verb or by adding *-s* or *-es* to the end.

'He <u>gets</u> up very early every morning.'

subordinate clause a clause which adds details to the main clause of the sentence but cannot be used as a sentence by itself

'<u>When I finish my homework</u>, I will go and meet my friends.'

suffix a word or syllable placed at the end of a word to modify its meaning. For example, in the word 'tasteless', the suffix *-less* makes the word 'tasteless' mean 'with no taste'.

superlative superlative adjectives and adverbs are used to compare and contrast three or more people, things or actions. The superlative shows which is greatest or most, and is generally formed by adding *-est* or *-st*.

'Cheetahs are the <u>fastest</u> land animals.'

syllable a unit of pronunciation that forms part of or the whole of a word. English words consist of one or more syllables. Each syllable always contains one speech vowel. This may have one or more speech consonants before and/or after it.

1 syllable – 'house', 2 syllables – 'kettle', 3 syllables – 'butterfly'

synonym a word or phrase that means exactly or nearly the same as another word or phrase in the same language. For example, the verb 'shut' is a synonym of the verb 'close'.

verb phrase a group of words, including the main verb and any other linking verbs or modifiers, that act as a sentence's verb

'My brother <u>is studying</u> in his room.'